THE ENTREPRENEUR'S PLAYBOOK

LAUNCHING YOUR BUSINESS WITH CONFIDENCE

DR. MINAKSHI BANSAL

DEDICATION

This book is dedicated to the dreamers and doers, those who dare to turn their visions into reality. To the entrepreneurs who face challenges with resilience and embrace opportunities with enthusiasm, this is for you. To my family and friends, whose unwavering support and belief in my journey have been my guiding light, thank you for your endless encouragement. To my mentors and colleagues, who have shared their wisdom and experiences, your insights have shaped this work profoundly. Finally, to every aspiring entrepreneur, may this book be your companion in navigating the path to success, offering guidance, inspiration, and confidence as you embark on your own remarkable journey.

Contents

Contents

Prayer

"Om Bhadram Karnebhih Shrinuyama Devah

Bhadram Pashyemakshabhiryajatrah

Sthirairangais Tushtuvamsastanubhih

Vyashema Devahitam Yadayuh

Svasti Na Indro Vriddhashravah

Svasti Nah Pusha Vishwavedah

Svasti Nastarkshyo Arishtanemih

Svasti No Brihaspatir Dadhatu

Om Shantih Shantih Shantih"

This mantra is a prayer for universal well-being, invoking the blessings of various deities for protection, health, and happiness. It emphasizes the importance of experiencing the auspicious through all senses and living a life aligned with divine purpose. The repetition of "Shantih" at the end signifies a deep desire for peace in the individual, the environment, and the universe at large. This mantra is often recited as a prayer for peace, prosperity, and the physical and spiritual well-being of all beings.

ﮮﮮﮮ

About The Author

This book represents the culmination of extensive research and meticulous analysis, incorporating a diverse range of sources, including numerous books, scholarly studies, and personal experiences. Additionally, I have scoured various websites to gather relevant information and data essential for the compilation of this work. I have taken every precaution to ensure the accuracy of the information presented and have diligently cited all sources to acknowledge their contributions.

From her earliest days, Minakshi was distinguished by an insatiable appetite for reading. Her literary universe was inhabited by characters and narratives that spanned ethical tales, motivational and inspirational stories, and the mythic parables imbued with life lessons. This voracious reading habit was not merely for personal edification but was driven by a desire to distill and disseminate the essence of these narratives to foster the development of students and peers alike. She was particularly captivated by the lives and teachings of historical figures and spiritual leaders such as Adi Shankaracharya, Swami Vivekananda, Dr. APJ Abdul Kalam, Mahamana Pandit Madan Mohan Malviya, Mahatma Gandhi, Sardar Vallabhai Patel, and Vinoba Bhave, among others. Their philosophies and life stories fueled her ambition to embody their ideals of resilience, selflessness, and relentless pursuit of knowledge.

Dr. Minakshi's academic and practical engagement with psychology has been equally noteworthy. As a research scholar, her focus has been on exploring the intricate tapestry of the human psyche, aiming to unlock the potential for psychological well-being and societal harmony. Her scholarly work is complemented by her active involvement in social work, where she employs her academic insights to make tangible differences in the lives of the underprivileged. Her endeavours in social work are characterized by an innovative approach that combines traditional wisdom with contemporary psychological practices to address the multifaceted challenges faced by these communities.

Her artistic talents, another facet of her diverse capabilities, are not merely a personal passion but also serve as a medium through which she communicates and connects with others. Her art, rich in symbolism and emotional depth, reflects her philosophical inquiries and social concerns, offering viewers a glimpse into the breadth of her intellect and the depth of her compassion.

In addition to her contributions to the arts and social sciences, Dr. Minakshi has embraced the healing arts of Pranic Healing, mastering the techniques developed by Master Choa Kok Sui. This practice, which focuses on the manipulation of Prana or life energy to heal the body and aura, has been both a personal journey of discovery and a means through which she extends her healing touch to others. Her proficiency in Pranic Healing is complemented by her advocacy and teaching of various forms of meditation aimed at rejuvenation, personal betterment, and the cultivation of harmony within individuals and communities alike.

Dr. Minakshi's life is a narrative of relentless pursuit, not just of personal achievement but of the upliftment and empowerment of society at large. Her diverse interests and talents—spanning the arts, literature, psychology, and the healing practices—converge on a singular path of service. She embodies the spirit of the luminaries who inspired her, channelling their legacy through her actions and teachings. Through her books, art, and social initiatives, she continues to inspire a new generation to embark on their own journeys of self-discovery, resilience, and altruism.

Her commitment to social betterment, particularly her focus on uplifting underprivileged children, reflects a deep understanding of the transformative potential of education and personal development. By integrating her knowledge of psychology, her artistic sensibilities, and her healing practices, Dr. Bansal has developed a holistic approach to social work that addresses both the immediate needs and the long-term well-being of the communities she serves.

As an author, Dr. Minakshi's writings offer a blend of inspirational insights, practical wisdom, and reflective contemplations drawn from her extensive reading and life experiences. Her books serve as a guide for those seeking to navigate the complexities of life with grace, resilience, and purpose. Through her narratives, she extends an invitation to her readers to explore the depths of their own potential and to contribute meaningfully to the collective well-being of society.

In Dr. Minakshi Bansal, we find a remarkable synthesis of the artist, the scholar, the healer, and the social activist. Her life's work stands as a beacon of hope and a source of inspiration for individuals seeking to make a difference in the world. Her story is a compelling reminder of the power of individual action, rooted in compassion and driven by a profound commitment to the betterment of humanity. Dr. Minakshi's legacy is not just in the tangible outcomes of her efforts but in the enduring spirit of inquiry, empathy, and service that she embodies.

ppp

Preface

As I embarked on my journey to write this book, I reflected deeply on my own experiences and the multitude of lessons learned throughout my entrepreneurial endeavors. The path to entrepreneurship is exhilarating yet fraught with challenges, and it is through these experiences that one grows and learns. I was driven by a desire to share these insights and practical advice, to provide a comprehensive guide for aspiring entrepreneurs who are ready to launch their business with confidence.

Entrepreneurship is more than just starting a business; it is about turning visions into reality, navigating uncertainties, and creating value. The process requires not only a sound business idea but also resilience, adaptability, and a strategic approach. Throughout my career, I have witnessed the highs and lows of building a business from the ground up. I have celebrated successes and weathered failures, each teaching me invaluable lessons that I wish to impart to you.

Reflecting on my early days as an entrepreneur, I remember the excitement and trepidation that came with my first venture. The thrill of creating something new was palpable, yet the fear of the unknown loomed large. I quickly realized that while passion and enthusiasm are essential, they must be complemented by thorough preparation and a clear strategy. This realization was a turning point, guiding me to approach entrepreneurship with a balanced perspective of creativity and pragmatism.

One of the foundational steps in this journey is crafting a clear and compelling vision. A vision serves as the guiding star, providing direction and purpose. It is what drives you forward during challenging times and inspires others to join you on your mission.

My own vision has evolved over the years, shaped by experiences and insights gained along the way. I have learned that a vision must be both aspirational and grounded in reality, offering a roadmap for where you want to go and how you plan to get there.

Market research is another critical aspect that cannot be overlooked. Understanding your target audience, identifying market needs, and analyzing competitors provide the insights necessary to refine your business idea. I have often found that the more you know about your market, the better positioned you are to offer solutions that resonate with your customers. This knowledge not only informs your product development but also shapes your marketing and sales strategies, ensuring that your efforts are aligned with market demands.

Developing a robust business plan is akin to building the foundation of a house. It outlines your business model, strategies, and financial projections, serving as a blueprint for your entrepreneurial journey. My early business plans were rudimentary, but with each new venture, I learned the importance of detailed planning. A well-crafted business plan helps secure funding, guides your actions, and measures progress. It transforms abstract ideas into a structured, actionable framework.

Navigating the legal landscape is often a daunting task for new entrepreneurs. Legal foundations such as business registration, intellectual property protection, and regulatory compliance are crucial for establishing a secure and credible business structure.

I remember the confusion and frustration of dealing with legal intricacies in my initial ventures. However, seeking professional advice and understanding these elements early on can prevent future complications and ensure that your business operates smoothly and legally.

Securing funding is one of the most challenging aspects of launching a business. The process of exploring various financing options, from personal savings and angel investors to venture capital and crowdfunding, requires careful consideration. Each funding source has its own set of advantages and considerations.

My journey has taught me the importance of financial management, not only in securing initial capital but also in ensuring the long-term sustainability of the business. Budgeting, forecasting, and cash flow management are critical components of maintaining financial health.

Building a memorable brand identity is essential for differentiating your business and establishing a strong market presence. Your brand is more than just a logo or tagline; it is the essence of what your business stands for. Crafting a cohesive visual identity, creating a compelling brand message, and consistently communicating your brand across all touchpoints are key to building a loyal customer base. In my experience, a strong brand not only attracts customers but also fosters trust and loyalty, driving long-term success.

In today's digital age, establishing a robust online presence is imperative. A professional website, active social media profiles, and effective digital marketing strategies are essential for reaching and engaging with your target audience. I have seen firsthand how leveraging digital tools can amplify your reach and enhance customer engagement. SEO, content marketing, and social media advertising are powerful tactics that can drive traffic and build your online reputation.

Product development is the heart of any business. Bringing your idea to life involves ideation, design, prototyping, testing, and refining your product to meet customer needs and market demands. It is a dynamic process that requires creativity, attention to detail, and a customer-centric approach. Throughout my career, I have learned the importance of continuous innovation and improvement, ensuring that your product evolves to stay relevant and competitive.

Setting the right pricing strategy is crucial for positioning your product in the market and ensuring profitability. Pricing decisions should consider factors such as cost, value to the customer, competition, and market conditions. My experiences have taught me that pricing is both an art and a science, requiring a deep understanding of your market and a strategic approach to balance affordability and profitability.

Marketing and sales are the engines that drive business growth. Effective marketing tactics involve a mix of digital and traditional channels, content marketing, social media engagement, email marketing, and paid advertising. Converting leads into customers through effective sales techniques requires clear communication, relationship building, and strategic closing methods. Providing excellent customer service is key to building loyalty and retention, creating a positive customer experience, and fostering long-term relationships.

Operational efficiency is essential for sustaining business growth. Streamlining processes, optimizing workflows, and leveraging technology can significantly enhance productivity and reduce costs. My journey has highlighted the importance of continuous assessment and optimization, ensuring that operations are efficient and scalable.

Building a strong team is also crucial for achieving business goals. Effective hiring, training, and management practices create a motivated and high-performing team that drives success.

Financial management is a cornerstone of business sustainability.

Careful planning, budgeting, forecasting, and monitoring of financial performance are essential for maintaining profitability and growth. Effective cash flow management, investment decisions, cost control, and risk management are critical components of financial health.

Scaling up the business involves strategic planning, resource management, and maintaining quality and core values as you expand operations and enter new markets.

Overcoming challenges and navigating obstacles with resilience is an inevitable part of the entrepreneurial journey. Identifying problems, developing solutions, and fostering a resilient organizational culture are key to overcoming challenges. Effective communication, adaptability, and continuous improvement are essential for navigating obstacles and emerging stronger.

Innovation and adaptation are crucial for staying ahead in the market. Cultivating a culture of creativity, embracing new technologies, and continuously learning are essential for driving innovation. Adaptation requires flexibility and agility, enabling businesses to respond effectively to market changes and seize opportunities.

Reflecting on success, celebrating milestones, and planning ahead are essential components of a dynamic and forward-thinking business strategy. Celebrating milestones acknowledges the hard work and dedication of the team, boosts morale, and strengthens the organizational culture. Reflection provides insights for continuous improvement, while planning ahead ensures that the organization remains proactive, aligned with its long-term vision, and prepared for future challenges and opportunities.

As I conclude this preface, I am reminded of the resilience, determination, and passion that define the entrepreneurial spirit.

The journey is not always easy, but it is immensely rewarding. Each step, each challenge, and each success contributes to a richer and more fulfilling experience. My hope is that this book serves as a valuable guide, providing practical insights and inspiration to help you navigate your own entrepreneurial journey with confidence.

Whether you are just starting out or looking to scale your business, remember that success is not a destination but a continuous journey of growth, learning, and innovation. Embrace the challenges, celebrate the milestones, and always look ahead with optimism and determination.

Dr. Minakshi Bansal
Social Activist
Ahmedabad, Gujarat, Bharat

ONE

INTRODUCTION TO ENTREPRENEURSHIP: UNLEASHING YOUR POTENTIAL

Entrepreneurship is a journey that begins with the spark of an idea and evolves into the creation of a thriving business. It is the process of designing, launching, and running a new business, often initially a small business, offering a product, process, or service for sale or hire. The potential within each aspiring entrepreneur is immense, waiting to be unleashed through dedication, innovation, and perseverance. Understanding the core of entrepreneurship and the mindset required to succeed is essential for anyone looking to embark on this journey.

At its core, entrepreneurship is about recognizing opportunities and creating value. It involves identifying unmet needs or underserved markets and developing solutions that address these gaps. This process begins with an idea, often inspired by personal experiences, industry trends, or observed challenges. However, an idea alone is not enough; it requires a vision to transform it into a viable business concept. Vision is the ability to see beyond the immediate and to imagine the future impact of your idea. It is this vision that drives entrepreneurs to take risks, overcome obstacles, and pursue their goals relentlessly.

The journey of entrepreneurship is not for the faint-hearted. It demands a unique blend of qualities, including creativity, resilience, adaptability, and a strong work ethic. Creativity is crucial as it allows entrepreneurs to think outside the box and develop innovative solutions. It is the engine that drives new ideas and approaches, enabling businesses to stand out in a crowded marketplace. Resilience is equally important, as the entrepreneurial path is fraught with challenges and setbacks. The ability to bounce back from failures, learn from mistakes, and keep moving forward is what sets successful entrepreneurs apart from those who give up.

Adaptability is another critical trait for entrepreneurs. The business landscape is constantly changing, influenced by technological advancements, market dynamics, and consumer preferences. Entrepreneurs must be flexible and willing to pivot their strategies in response to these changes. This requires staying informed about industry trends, being open to feedback, and continuously seeking ways to improve and innovate. A strong work ethic is the foundation of any successful entrepreneurial endeavor. Building a business from the ground up requires long hours, dedication, and a relentless pursuit of excellence. Entrepreneurs must be willing to put in the hard work and make sacrifices to achieve their goals.

One of the first steps in unleashing your entrepreneurial potential is to cultivate an entrepreneurial mindset. This mindset is characterized by a proactive approach, a willingness to take calculated risks, and a focus on long-term goals. It involves shifting from a fixed mindset, where abilities are seen as static, to a growth mindset, where abilities can be developed through dedication and hard work. Embracing a growth mindset allows entrepreneurs to see challenges as opportunities for growth and to persist in the face of adversity.

Networking and building relationships are also essential components of entrepreneurship. Surrounding yourself with a supportive network of mentors, peers, and advisors can provide valuable guidance, insights, and encouragement. Mentors can offer advice based on their own experiences, helping you navigate the complexities of starting and running a business. Peers who share similar challenges can provide support and camaraderie, while advisors with specialized expertise can offer strategic advice in areas such as finance, marketing, and operations.

Another crucial aspect of unleashing your entrepreneurial potential is continuous learning and self-improvement. The business world is dynamic, and staying ahead requires a commitment to lifelong learning. This can be achieved through formal education, such as attending business courses or workshops, as well as informal learning, such as reading industry publications, listening to podcasts, and following thought leaders. Staying curious and open to new ideas will enable you to adapt to changing circumstances and seize new opportunities.

Identifying and validating your business idea is a critical step in the entrepreneurial journey. This involves conducting thorough market research to understand your target audience, competitors, and industry trends. Market research helps you identify unmet needs, assess demand for your product or service, and refine your value proposition. It also provides insights into potential challenges and opportunities, allowing you to make informed decisions and develop a viable business model.

Once you have validated your business idea, developing a comprehensive business plan is essential. A business plan serves as a roadmap, outlining your business objectives, strategies, and financial projections. It helps you stay focused on your goals, allocate resources effectively, and measure your progress. A well-crafted business plan also serves as a valuable tool when seeking funding from investors or lenders, as it demonstrates your commitment and preparedness.

Securing funding is often one of the biggest challenges for aspiring entrepreneurs. There are various sources of funding available, including personal savings, loans, grants, and equity investments. Each funding option has its pros and cons, and it's important to choose the one that aligns with your business needs and goals. Personal savings and bootstrapping allow you to retain full control of your business but may limit your financial resources. Loans and grants can provide much-needed capital but often come with stringent requirements and repayment obligations. Equity investments offer significant funding but require giving up a portion of ownership and control. Carefully evaluating your funding options and developing a solid financial plan will help you secure the necessary resources to launch and grow your business.

Building a strong brand is another key element of entrepreneurial success. Your brand represents your business's identity and values, and it differentiates you from your competitors. Developing a compelling brand involves creating a unique value proposition, designing a memorable logo, and crafting a consistent brand message. It also requires understanding your target audience and tailoring your brand to resonate with their needs and preferences. A strong brand not only attracts customers but also builds trust and loyalty, which are essential for long-term success.

In today's digital age, establishing an online presence is crucial for any business. This involves creating a professional website, engaging on social media platforms, and utilizing digital marketing strategies to reach your target audience. A well-designed website serves as your business's virtual storefront, providing information about your products or services, showcasing your brand, and facilitating online transactions. Social media platforms offer valuable opportunities to connect with your audience, build relationships, and promote your business. Leveraging digital marketing techniques, such as search engine optimization (SEO), content marketing, and email campaigns, can help you increase your visibility, drive traffic to your website, and generate leads.

Product development is a critical phase in the entrepreneurial journey, as it involves transforming your idea into a tangible product or service. This process requires a deep understanding of your target market's needs and preferences, as well as a commitment to quality and innovation. Developing a minimum viable product (MVP) is a common strategy for testing your concept with early adopters and gathering feedback. An MVP is a simplified version of your product that includes only the core features necessary to meet the needs of your target audience. By launching an MVP, you can validate your idea, identify areas for improvement, and iterate on your product based on real-world feedback.

Pricing your product or service effectively is another critical aspect of entrepreneurship. Setting the right price involves balancing several factors, including production costs, market demand, competitor pricing, and perceived value. Pricing strategies can vary widely, from cost-plus pricing, where you add a markup to your production costs, to value-based pricing, where you set prices based on the perceived value to the customer. Conducting market research and analyzing your competitors' pricing can provide valuable insights into pricing your product competitively and profitably.

Marketing and sales are the lifeblood of any business, as they drive customer acquisition and revenue growth. Developing a comprehensive marketing strategy involves identifying your target audience, defining your unique selling proposition (USP), and selecting the right marketing channels. Effective marketing tactics can include content marketing, social media marketing, influencer partnerships, and paid advertising. Sales techniques, such as consultative selling, relationship building, and upselling, can help you convert leads into customers and increase your revenue. Providing excellent customer service and building strong relationships with your customers are essential for retaining their loyalty and encouraging repeat business.

Operational efficiency is critical for the success of any business, as it impacts your ability to deliver products or services consistently and cost-effectively. Streamlining your processes, optimizing your supply chain, and implementing effective project management practices can help you improve efficiency and reduce costs. Leveraging technology, such as automation tools and enterprise resource planning (ERP) systems, can also enhance your operational capabilities and enable you to scale your business more effectively.

Building a strong team is another essential component of entrepreneurial success. Hiring the right people, providing them with the necessary training and support, and fostering a positive work culture are crucial for building a high-performing team. Effective leadership and communication skills are essential for managing your team, setting clear expectations, and motivating your employees to achieve their best. Encouraging collaboration, recognizing and rewarding achievements, and providing opportunities for professional growth can help you build a cohesive and dedicated team.

Financial management is a critical aspect of running a successful business, as it ensures your business remains profitable and sustainable. This involves managing your cash flow, tracking your expenses, and preparing financial statements such as income statements, balance sheets, and cash flow statements. Implementing sound financial practices, such as budgeting, forecasting, and cost control, can help you make informed decisions and maintain financial stability. Seeking the advice of financial experts, such as accountants or financial advisors, can also provide valuable insights and guidance.

As your business grows, scaling up becomes a priority. Scaling involves expanding your operations, increasing your market reach, and growing your revenue while maintaining quality and efficiency. This requires careful planning, resource allocation, and strategic decision-making. Identifying new market opportunities, diversifying your product or service offerings, and investing in technology and infrastructure can help you scale your business sustainably.

Throughout the entrepreneurial journey, overcoming challenges is inevitable. Whether it's facing financial difficulties, dealing with competition, or navigating regulatory hurdles, resilience and problem-solving skills are essential. Viewing challenges as opportunities for growth, seeking advice from mentors and advisors, and maintaining a positive mindset can help you overcome obstacles and keep moving forward.

Innovation and adaptation are crucial for staying competitive in a dynamic business environment. Continuously seeking new ways to improve your products, services, and processes, staying informed about industry trends, and being open to change can help you stay ahead of the competition. Encouraging a culture of innovation within your team, fostering creativity, and embracing new technologies can also drive your business's growth and success.

Reflecting on your entrepreneurial journey, celebrating your achievements, and setting new goals are essential for long-term success. Taking the time to acknowledge your accomplishments, learning from your experiences, and planning for the future can help you stay motivated and focused on your vision. Setting new goals, both short-term and long-term, provides direction and purpose, ensuring your business continues to grow and thrive.

In conclusion, entrepreneurship is a challenging yet rewarding journey that requires a unique blend of qualities, a proactive mindset, and a commitment to continuous learning and improvement. By unleashing your potential, embracing innovation, and staying resilient in the face of challenges, you can transform your ideas into a thriving business and achieve your entrepreneurial dreams.

ᐅᐅᐅ

"Vision is the spark that ignites the journey of entrepreneurship. It guides your steps through the darkest paths. Believe in your vision, for it is the foundation of all success."

TWO

CRAFTING YOUR VISION: DEFINING YOUR BUSINESS IDEA

Crafting your vision and defining your business idea is the foundational step in the entrepreneurial journey. It is where inspiration meets strategy, and abstract concepts are transformed into actionable plans. This process requires introspection, market understanding, creativity, and a clear articulation of what you aim to achieve with your business. The vision you craft and the business idea you define will serve as the guiding star for all your entrepreneurial endeavors.

The first step in crafting your vision is to understand your motivations for starting a business. Reflect on what drives you and what you hope to accomplish. Are you motivated by a passion for a particular industry or a desire to solve a specific problem? Do you seek financial independence, or are you driven by the potential to make a social impact? Clarifying your motivations will help you align your business idea with your personal goals and values, ensuring that your venture is meaningful and fulfilling.

Once you have a clear understanding of your motivations, the next step is to identify a business idea that resonates with your vision. This often begins with brainstorming and exploring various possibilities. Look at your skills, experiences, and interests as potential sources of inspiration. What unique talents or expertise do you possess that could be the foundation of a business? Consider the challenges you have encountered in your personal or professional life and think about how you could address these issues through a business solution. Engaging in creative thinking exercises, such as mind mapping or brainstorming sessions with peers, can help generate a diverse range of ideas.

Market research is a crucial component of defining your business idea. It involves gathering and analyzing information about your target market, industry trends, and competitors. Understanding the needs, preferences, and behaviors of your potential customers is essential for developing a product or service that meets their demands. Start by identifying your target market segments and creating detailed customer personas. These personas should include demographic information, such as age, gender, income, and location, as well as psychographic details, such as interests, values, and lifestyle. By having a clear picture of your ideal customer, you can tailor your business idea to better serve their needs.

In addition to understanding your customers, it is important to analyze your competitors. Identify other businesses offering similar products or services and evaluate their strengths and weaknesses. What do they do well, and where do they fall short? How can you differentiate your business from theirs? Conducting a SWOT analysis (Strengths, Weaknesses, Opportunities, Threats) can provide valuable insights into your competitive landscape and help you identify opportunities for innovation and improvement.

As you refine your business idea, focus on creating a unique value proposition (UVP). Your UVP is the compelling reason why customers should choose your product or service over others in the market. It highlights the unique benefits and features that set your business apart and addresses the specific needs or pain points of your target audience. Crafting a strong UVP requires a deep understanding of your customers and a clear articulation of how your business adds value to their lives. This process often involves testing and validating your ideas through feedback from potential customers. Conduct surveys, interviews, or focus groups to gather insights and refine your UVP based on real-world input.

Defining your business idea also involves considering the practical aspects of bringing it to life. Evaluate the feasibility of your idea by assessing the resources required, including time, money, skills, and technology. Create a rough outline of your business model, detailing how your business will generate revenue, deliver value to customers, and operate efficiently. Consider different revenue streams, such as product sales, subscriptions, or service fees, and determine which aligns best with your business idea and target market. Assess the costs associated with launching and running your business, including production, marketing, distribution, and operational expenses. A clear understanding of the financial implications will help you determine the viability of your idea and plan accordingly.

Innovation plays a crucial role in defining a successful business idea. It involves finding new and creative ways to solve problems, improve processes, and deliver value to customers. Embrace a mindset of continuous improvement and be open to exploring unconventional approaches. Look for inspiration from other industries, emerging technologies, and market trends. Collaborate with others to generate fresh perspectives and ideas. Encourage a culture of innovation within your team, fostering an environment where creativity and experimentation are valued.

Once you have a well-defined business idea, it is important to articulate your vision clearly and compellingly. Your vision statement should be a concise and inspiring declaration of what you aim to achieve with your business. It should capture the essence of your business idea and convey your long-term goals and aspirations. A strong vision statement serves as a motivational tool, guiding your actions and decisions and inspiring others to support your venture. It provides a sense of direction and purpose, helping you stay focused on your objectives even in the face of challenges.

Your vision should be supported by a set of core values that reflect the principles and beliefs guiding your business. These values serve as the foundation for your company culture and influence how you interact with customers, employees, and stakeholders. Clearly defining your core values helps ensure consistency and integrity in your business practices and builds trust and credibility with your audience. Communicate your values through your branding, marketing, and customer interactions, and strive to embody them in everything you do.

Building a strong brand is an essential part of defining your business idea and crafting your vision. Your brand represents your business identity and sets the tone for how customers perceive you. It encompasses your company name, logo, tagline, visual elements, and overall messaging. A compelling brand communicates your unique value proposition and differentiates you from competitors. Invest time and effort in developing a brand that resonates with your target audience and reflects your vision and values. Ensure consistency in your branding across all touchpoints, from your website and social media profiles to your packaging and customer communications.

Developing a marketing strategy is another critical aspect of defining your business idea. Your marketing strategy outlines how you will reach and engage your target audience and promote your products or services. Start by identifying the most effective marketing channels for your business, such as social media, email marketing, content marketing, or paid advertising. Create a detailed plan for how you will use these channels to build awareness, generate leads, and drive conversions. Develop compelling marketing messages that highlight your unique value proposition and resonate with your audience's needs and desires. Continuously monitor and analyze the performance of your marketing efforts, and be prepared to adjust your strategy based on feedback and results.

Crafting your vision and defining your business idea is an ongoing process that requires flexibility and adaptability. As you move forward with your business, be open to feedback and willing to make adjustments as needed. Continuously evaluate your progress and reassess your goals and strategies to ensure alignment with your vision. Stay informed about industry trends, emerging technologies, and changes in customer preferences, and be ready to pivot your approach when necessary. Embrace a mindset of continuous learning and improvement, and seek opportunities to innovate and enhance your business.

Building a successful business also requires a strong support system. Surround yourself with mentors, advisors, and peers who can offer guidance, insights, and encouragement. Mentors can provide valuable advice based on their own experiences and help you navigate the complexities of entrepreneurship. Advisors with specialized expertise can offer strategic guidance in areas such as finance, marketing, and operations. Peers who share similar challenges and goals can provide support and camaraderie. Building a network of trusted individuals can help you stay motivated and focused on your vision.

As you work to bring your business idea to life, it is important to stay true to your vision and values. Maintain a clear sense of purpose and direction, and let your vision guide your decisions and actions. Stay committed to your goals, even in the face of challenges and setbacks. Remember that entrepreneurship is a journey, and success often requires perseverance and resilience. Celebrate your achievements along the way, and use them as motivation to keep moving forward.

In conclusion, crafting your vision and defining your business idea is a critical step in the entrepreneurial journey. It involves understanding your motivations, identifying a business idea that aligns with your vision, conducting thorough market research, and creating a unique value proposition. Practical considerations, such as evaluating feasibility and developing a business model, are essential for turning your idea into reality. Embracing innovation, articulating your vision clearly, and building a strong brand and marketing strategy are key components of defining a successful business idea. Staying flexible, seeking support, and staying true to your vision and values will help you navigate the challenges and achieve your entrepreneurial goals.

ᗰᗰᗰ

"Market research is the compass for your business. It reveals the landscape and helps you navigate with precision. Understanding your market is the key to unlocking potential."

THREE

MARKET RESEARCH: UNDERSTANDING YOUR AUDIENCE AND COMPETITORS

Market research is a fundamental component of building a successful business. It provides the insights necessary to understand your target audience and competitors, enabling you to make informed decisions and develop strategies that resonate with your customers. Understanding your audience involves identifying their needs, preferences, and behaviors, while analyzing competitors helps you identify gaps in the market and opportunities for differentiation. Together, these insights form the foundation of your business strategy, guiding product development, marketing, and overall business operations.

The first step in conducting market research is to define your target audience. This involves segmenting the market into distinct groups based on various criteria such as demographics, psychographics, geographic location, and behavior. Demographic segmentation includes factors like age, gender, income, education level, and occupation. Psychographic segmentation focuses on lifestyle, values, interests, and personality traits. Geographic segmentation considers the physical location of your audience, while behavioral segmentation looks at purchasing behavior, usage patterns, and brand loyalty. By understanding the different segments of your market, you can tailor your products, services, and marketing efforts to meet the specific needs and preferences of each group.

Once you have defined your target audience, creating detailed customer personas can further refine your understanding. Customer personas are fictional representations of your ideal customers, based on real data and insights. Each persona includes demographic and psychographic details, as well as specific goals, challenges, and buying behaviors. Developing these personas involves gathering data from various sources, such as surveys, interviews, focus groups, and social media analysis. Engaging with your audience directly and listening to their feedback can provide valuable insights into their motivations and pain points. By creating accurate and detailed personas, you can ensure that your business decisions are aligned with the needs and desires of your customers.

Understanding your audience also requires analyzing their behavior and preferences. This involves studying how they interact with your products or services, what influences their purchasing decisions, and what factors contribute to their loyalty. Analyzing customer feedback, reviews, and testimonials can reveal common themes and areas for improvement. Tracking metrics such as website traffic, social media engagement, and sales data can provide quantitative insights into customer behavior. By combining qualitative and quantitative data, you can develop a comprehensive understanding of your audience and identify opportunities to enhance their experience.

Competitor analysis is another critical aspect of market research. It involves identifying and evaluating the businesses that offer similar products or services and understanding their strengths and weaknesses. Start by creating a list of your direct and indirect competitors. Direct competitors are those that offer similar products or services to the same target audience, while indirect competitors may offer alternative solutions or operate in related markets. Once you have identified your competitors, gather information about their products, pricing, marketing strategies, and customer experiences. This can be done through various methods, such as visiting their websites, following their social media accounts, reading customer reviews, and analyzing industry reports.

A SWOT analysis (Strengths, Weaknesses, Opportunities, Threats) is a useful tool for organizing and evaluating the information gathered during competitor analysis. Identify the key strengths and weaknesses of each competitor, as well as the opportunities and threats they present to your business. Strengths may include factors such as brand reputation, product quality, customer loyalty, and distribution channels. Weaknesses could be areas where competitors are lacking, such as limited product features, poor customer service, or high prices. Opportunities may arise from market trends, technological advancements, or gaps in the market that your business can exploit. Threats could include new entrants to the market, changing consumer preferences, or regulatory changes.

By analyzing your competitors, you can identify what sets your business apart and develop strategies to differentiate yourself in the market. This could involve offering unique features, superior quality, competitive pricing, exceptional customer service, or innovative marketing campaigns. Understanding your competitors' strengths and weaknesses also allows you to anticipate their actions and respond proactively. For example, if a competitor is known for excellent customer service, you may focus on enhancing your own customer support to stay competitive. If a competitor is launching a new product, you can analyze its potential impact on your market and adjust your strategies accordingly.

Market research also involves analyzing broader industry trends and market dynamics. Understanding the external factors that influence your market, such as economic conditions, technological advancements, regulatory changes, and social trends, is essential for making informed business decisions. Industry reports, market research studies, and news articles can provide valuable insights into the current state of the market and future projections. Keeping up with industry trends allows you to identify emerging opportunities and potential challenges, enabling you to adapt your strategies and stay ahead of the competition.

Technology plays a significant role in modern market research, providing tools and platforms that enable more efficient and accurate data collection and analysis. Online surveys and questionnaires can reach a large audience quickly and provide valuable quantitative data. Social media listening tools allow you to monitor conversations and trends related to your industry, brand, and competitors. Web analytics tools track user behavior on your website, providing insights into what drives traffic and conversions. Customer relationship management (CRM) systems store and analyze customer data, helping you understand their interactions and preferences. Leveraging these technologies can enhance your market research efforts and provide deeper insights into your audience and competitors.

Effective market research requires a systematic and ongoing approach. It is not a one-time activity but a continuous process of gathering and analyzing data to stay informed about your market and make data-driven decisions. Regularly updating your market research helps you stay attuned to changes in customer preferences, emerging trends, and competitive dynamics. Establishing key performance indicators (KPIs) and tracking them over time can help you measure the effectiveness of your strategies and identify areas for improvement. By staying proactive and responsive to market changes, you can ensure that your business remains relevant and competitive.

Ethical considerations are also important in market research. Respecting the privacy and confidentiality of your customers and research participants is paramount. Ensure that you obtain informed consent when collecting data and be transparent about how the data will be used. Avoid deceptive or manipulative practices, such as misleading survey questions or biased interpretations of data. Adhering to ethical standards builds trust with your audience and enhances the credibility of your research findings.

The insights gained from market research should be integrated into your overall business strategy. Use the data to inform product development, marketing, sales, and customer service decisions. For example, if market research reveals a high demand for a particular feature, prioritize its development and highlight it in your marketing campaigns. If customer feedback indicates dissatisfaction with a certain aspect of your service, take steps to address the issue and improve the customer experience. Aligning your business strategy with market research insights ensures that your decisions are grounded in real-world data and reflect the needs and preferences of your audience.

Incorporating market research into your marketing strategy is particularly important. Understanding your audience's preferences and behaviors allows you to create targeted and effective marketing campaigns. Tailor your messaging to resonate with your customer personas and address their specific needs and pain points. Choose the marketing channels that your audience prefers and optimize your content for those platforms. Monitor the performance of your campaigns and use the data to refine your approach and maximize your return on investment. By leveraging market research in your marketing efforts, you can build stronger connections with your audience and drive higher engagement and conversions.

Market research also plays a crucial role in risk management. By identifying potential threats and challenges early on, you can develop strategies to mitigate risks and protect your business. For example, if market research indicates a declining trend in demand for your product, you can explore new markets or diversify your product offerings. If regulatory changes pose a threat to your industry, you can stay informed and adapt your business practices to comply with new regulations. Proactively addressing risks based on market research insights helps you navigate uncertainties and maintain business stability.

Collaboration and communication are essential for effective market research. Involve key stakeholders, such as team members, partners, and advisors, in the research process to gather diverse perspectives and insights. Share your findings and analysis with your team to ensure that everyone is aligned and informed. Use the insights from market research to foster a culture of data-driven decision-making within your organization. Encouraging collaboration and open communication enhances the quality of your research and ensures that insights are effectively translated into action.

Investing in market research can provide a significant competitive advantage. Businesses that understand their audience and competitors are better positioned to create products and services that meet customer needs, develop effective marketing strategies, and make informed business decisions. Market research helps you identify opportunities for innovation, differentiate your business, and build strong customer relationships. It enables you to stay ahead of market trends, anticipate changes, and adapt proactively. By prioritizing market research, you can build a resilient and agile business that thrives in a dynamic and competitive landscape.

In conclusion, market research is a vital component of building a successful business. It involves understanding your target audience, analyzing competitors, and staying informed about industry trends and market dynamics. By defining your audience and creating detailed customer personas, you can tailor your products, services, and marketing efforts to meet their specific needs and preferences. Competitor analysis helps you identify gaps in the market and opportunities for differentiation, while industry analysis provides insights into broader market trends. Leveraging technology, maintaining ethical standards, and adopting a systematic and ongoing approach to market research ensures that your business remains relevant and competitive. Integrating market research insights into your overall business strategy enhances decision-making, risk management, and marketing effectiveness. By investing in market research, you can build a data-driven and customer-centric business that thrives in a dynamic and competitive environment.

▷▷▷

"A robust business plan is your roadmap to success. It transforms ideas into actionable strategies. Planning is not just about predicting the future, but shaping it."

FOUR

BUILDING A BUSINESS PLAN: STRUCTURING YOUR PATH TO SUCCESS

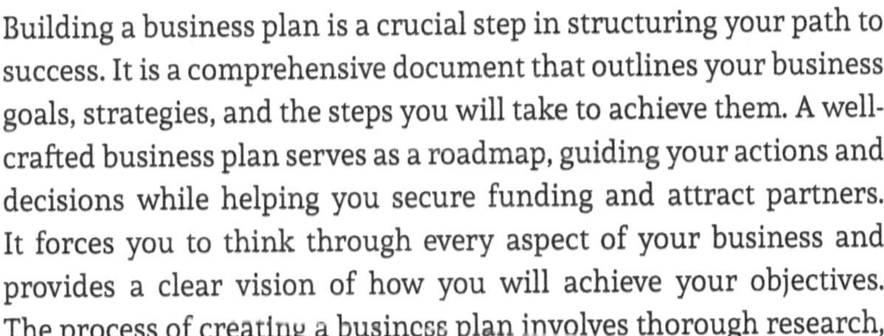

Building a business plan is a crucial step in structuring your path to success. It is a comprehensive document that outlines your business goals, strategies, and the steps you will take to achieve them. A well-crafted business plan serves as a roadmap, guiding your actions and decisions while helping you secure funding and attract partners. It forces you to think through every aspect of your business and provides a clear vision of how you will achieve your objectives. The process of creating a business plan involves thorough research, strategic thinking, and detailed planning.

The first step in building a business plan is to define your business concept. This involves clearly articulating what your business is about, what products or services you will offer, and what market needs you aim to address. Your business concept should be concise yet comprehensive, providing a clear overview of your business idea. This section of your business plan sets the stage for the rest of the document, giving readers a snapshot of your vision and goals. It is important to convey your passion and enthusiasm for your business while ensuring that your concept is grounded in market realities.

Next, conduct a detailed market analysis to understand the industry landscape, target market, and competitive environment. This involves researching market trends, customer needs, and competitor offerings. The goal is to gather enough information to make informed decisions about your business strategy and position your company for success. Start by identifying the size and growth potential of your market. Analyze demographic and psychographic data to understand your target customers better. Identify key trends and drivers in your industry, such as technological advancements, regulatory changes, or shifts in consumer behavior. This analysis will help you identify opportunities and threats in the market, allowing you to develop strategies to capitalize on the former and mitigate the latter.

A thorough competitive analysis is also essential. Identify your direct and indirect competitors and evaluate their strengths and weaknesses. Look at their products, pricing, marketing strategies, and customer reviews. Understanding your competitors' strategies will help you identify gaps in the market and develop a unique value proposition. It will also enable you to anticipate competitive actions and respond proactively. Use tools like SWOT analysis (Strengths, Weaknesses, Opportunities, Threats) to organize your findings and gain a clear understanding of your competitive position.

With a solid understanding of the market and competitive landscape, the next step is to define your business strategy. This involves outlining your long-term goals and the steps you will take to achieve them. Your business strategy should address key areas such as product development, marketing, sales, operations, and financial management. It should provide a clear path to achieving your business objectives, with specific, measurable, achievable, relevant, and time-bound (SMART) goals. For example, if your goal is to achieve a certain level of revenue within the first year, outline the specific actions you will take to reach that goal, such as launching new products, expanding into new markets, or increasing marketing efforts.

Product development is a critical component of your business strategy. This involves outlining the features and benefits of your products or services and how they meet the needs of your target market. Provide details on the development process, including research and development, prototyping, testing, and production. Highlight any unique or innovative aspects of your products that set them apart from competitors. Also, address any potential challenges in the product development process and how you plan to overcome them. A clear and detailed product development plan demonstrates that you have thought through every aspect of bringing your product to market.

Marketing and sales strategies are also essential components of your business plan. Your marketing strategy should outline how you will reach and engage your target audience, build brand awareness, and drive sales. Identify the marketing channels you will use, such as social media, content marketing, email marketing, or paid advertising. Provide details on your messaging and positioning, and how you will differentiate your brand from competitors. Outline your sales strategy, including your sales process, pricing, and distribution channels. Address any potential challenges in your marketing and sales efforts and how you plan to overcome them. A well-defined marketing and sales strategy shows that you have a clear plan for attracting and retaining customers.

Operations and management are another critical area of your business plan. This section should outline how your business will operate on a day-to-day basis, including production, logistics, and supply chain management. Provide details on your organizational structure, including key roles and responsibilities. Highlight any key personnel and their qualifications, and explain how their expertise will contribute to the success of your business. Address any potential operational challenges and how you plan to mitigate them. A clear and detailed operations plan demonstrates that you have thought through the practical aspects of running your business.

Financial management is a crucial component of your business plan, as it provides a clear picture of your business's financial health and viability. This section should include detailed financial projections, such as income statements, balance sheets, and cash flow statements. Provide realistic revenue and expense forecasts, and explain the assumptions behind your projections. Highlight any key financial metrics, such as gross margin, net profit margin, and return on investment. Address any potential financial risks and how you plan to mitigate them. A clear and detailed financial plan shows that you have a realistic understanding of your business's financial needs and how you plan to achieve profitability.

Securing funding is often a critical step in bringing your business plan to life. This section should outline your funding requirements, including how much capital you need, how you plan to use the funds, and the types of funding you are seeking. Provide details on your funding strategy, including potential sources of capital, such as personal savings, loans, grants, or equity investments. Highlight any key milestones or achievements that demonstrate your business's potential for success. Address any potential challenges in securing funding and how you plan to overcome them. A clear and compelling funding strategy shows that you have a realistic understanding of your financial needs and a plan for securing the necessary capital.

Risk management is another important aspect of your business plan. This involves identifying potential risks and developing strategies to mitigate them. Consider risks related to market conditions, competition, operations, finance, and regulatory changes. Outline your risk management strategies, such as diversifying your product offerings, building strong relationships with suppliers, or maintaining a healthy cash reserve. Address any potential challenges in managing risks and how you plan to overcome them. A clear and comprehensive risk management plan demonstrates that you have thought through potential challenges and are prepared to address them proactively.

Building a business plan is an iterative process that requires continuous review and refinement. As you gather more information and gain new insights, update your business plan to reflect any changes in your strategy or market conditions. Seek feedback from trusted advisors, mentors, and industry experts to ensure that your plan is realistic and achievable. Regularly reviewing and updating your business plan helps you stay focused on your goals and adapt to changing circumstances.

A well-crafted business plan is not only a valuable tool for securing funding and attracting partners but also a strategic guide for your business. It provides a clear vision of your goals and the steps you will take to achieve them. It forces you to think through every aspect of your business and make informed decisions. It also serves as a benchmark for measuring your progress and adjusting your strategies as needed.

In summary, building a business plan involves defining your business concept, conducting a detailed market analysis, developing a comprehensive business strategy, outlining your product development, marketing and sales, operations, and financial management plans, securing funding, and managing risks. It requires thorough research, strategic thinking, and detailed planning. A well-crafted business plan provides a clear roadmap for achieving your business goals and sets the stage for long-term success. By investing the time and effort to create a comprehensive and realistic business plan, you can ensure that your business is well-positioned for success and equipped to navigate the challenges and opportunities of the market.

ÞÞÞ

"Funding is the lifeblood of any venture. Securing it requires strategy, persistence, and a clear vision. Financial health is essential for sustaining growth and innovation."

FIVE

LEGAL FOUNDATIONS: REGISTERING AND PROTECTING YOUR BUSINESS

Establishing a solid legal foundation for your business is crucial for its long-term success. This involves registering your business, complying with regulations, protecting your intellectual property, and ensuring that you operate within the law. By addressing these legal considerations early on, you can avoid potential legal issues and create a strong foundation for your business to thrive.

The first step in establishing your business's legal foundation is choosing the right legal structure. The legal structure you select will affect your liability, taxes, and the ability to raise capital. The most common legal structures for businesses include sole proprietorships, partnerships, limited liability companies (LLCs), and corporations.

A sole proprietorship is the simplest and most common form of business structure. It is owned and operated by one individual, and there is no legal distinction between the owner and the business. This means that the owner is personally liable for all business debts and obligations. Sole proprietorships are easy to establish and have minimal regulatory requirements. However, the lack of liability protection can be a significant drawback.

Partnerships are similar to sole proprietorships but involve two or more individuals who share ownership of the business. There are two main types of partnerships: general partnerships and limited partnerships. In a general partnership, all partners share equal responsibility for the business's debts and obligations. In a limited partnership, there are both general partners and limited partners. General partners manage the business and are personally liable for its debts, while limited partners contribute capital but have limited liability. Partnerships can benefit from pooled resources and expertise, but personal liability and potential conflicts between partners are important considerations.

A limited liability company (LLC) is a popular business structure that combines the benefits of a corporation and a partnership. LLCs provide limited liability protection to their owners, known as members, meaning that members are not personally liable for the business's debts and obligations. LLCs offer flexibility in management and taxation, as they can choose to be taxed as a sole proprietorship, partnership, or corporation. The ease of setting up and operating an LLC, along with the liability protection it offers, makes it an attractive option for many entrepreneurs.

Corporations are more complex business structures that provide the strongest liability protection to their owners, known as shareholders. There are two main types of corporations: C corporations and S corporations. C corporations are separate legal entities from their owners and are subject to corporate income tax. Shareholders are not personally liable for the corporation's debts, and profits are distributed as dividends. S corporations, on the other hand, are pass-through entities, meaning that profits and losses are passed through to shareholders and reported on their personal tax returns. S corporations offer liability protection and potential tax benefits but have more regulatory requirements and restrictions on ownership.

Once you have chosen the appropriate legal structure for your business, the next step is to register your business with the relevant authorities. This typically involves registering your business name, obtaining necessary licenses and permits, and registering for taxes.

Registering your business name is an important step in establishing your brand identity and ensuring that your business operates legally. The process for registering a business name varies depending on your location and legal structure. In many cases, you will need to register your business name with your state's business registration office or local government. Conduct a name search to ensure that your chosen name is not already in use by another business. If you plan to operate under a different name than your legal business name, you may need to file a "doing business as" (DBA) registration.

Obtaining the necessary licenses and permits is another critical step in the registration process. The types of licenses and permits required for your business will depend on your industry, location, and the nature of your operations. Common licenses and permits include business licenses, professional licenses, health permits, and zoning permits. Research the specific requirements for your industry and location, and ensure that you comply with all applicable regulations. Failure to obtain the necessary licenses and permits can result in fines, legal penalties, and the closure of your business.

Registering for taxes is an essential part of establishing your business's legal foundation. This involves obtaining an Employer Identification Number (EIN) from the Internal Revenue Service (IRS) if you plan to hire employees or operate as a corporation or partnership. Your EIN is used to identify your business for tax purposes and is required for filing tax returns, opening a business bank account, and applying for business licenses. In addition to federal taxes, you may also need to register for state and local taxes, such as sales tax, payroll tax, and property tax. Consult with a tax professional to ensure that you comply with all tax registration requirements and understand your tax obligations.

Protecting your intellectual property is another critical aspect of establishing a solid legal foundation for your business. Intellectual property (IP) refers to creations of the mind, such as inventions, trademarks, copyrights, and trade secrets. Protecting your IP ensures that you have exclusive rights to your creations and can prevent others from using, copying, or profiting from your work without your permission.

Patents protect new inventions and grant the inventor exclusive rights to make, use, and sell the invention for a specified period, typically 20 years. There are three main types of patents: utility patents, design patents, and plant patents. Utility patents cover new and useful processes, machines, or compositions of matter. Design patents protect the ornamental design of a functional item. Plant patents are granted for new and distinct varieties of plants that have been asexually reproduced. To obtain a patent, you must file a patent application with the United States Patent and Trademark Office (USPTO) and meet the requirements for patentability.

Trademarks protect words, phrases, symbols, or designs that distinguish your goods or services from those of others. A trademark grants you exclusive rights to use the mark in connection with your products or services and helps prevent others from using a similar mark that could cause confusion among consumers. To protect your trademark, you can register it with the USPTO. Registration provides several benefits, including legal presumption of ownership, nationwide protection, and the ability to bring legal action against infringers. Conduct a trademark search to ensure that your chosen mark is not already in use, and consider working with a trademark attorney to navigate the registration process.

Copyrights protect original works of authorship, such as literary, musical, artistic, and dramatic works. A copyright grants the creator exclusive rights to reproduce, distribute, perform, and display the work, as well as to create derivative works. Copyright protection is automatic upon the creation of the work, but registering your copyright with the U.S. Copyright Office provides additional legal benefits, such as the ability to bring a lawsuit for infringement and to recover statutory damages and attorney's fees. To register a copyright, you must submit an application, a copy of the work, and a filing fee to the U.S. Copyright Office.

Trade secrets protect confidential business information that provides a competitive advantage, such as formulas, processes, or customer lists. Unlike patents and trademarks, trade secrets are not registered with a government agency. Instead, protection is maintained through confidentiality agreements and internal security measures. To protect your trade secrets, implement policies and procedures to limit access to the information and require employees, contractors, and business partners to sign non-disclosure agreements (NDAs).

In addition to protecting your intellectual property, it is important to ensure that your business complies with all relevant regulations and laws. This includes labor laws, environmental regulations, consumer protection laws, and industry-specific regulations.

Compliance with these laws is essential for avoiding legal penalties and maintaining a positive reputation.

Labor laws govern the relationship between employers and employees, covering areas such as wages, working hours, health and safety, and anti-discrimination. Ensure that you comply with federal, state, and local labor laws by paying employees at least the minimum wage, providing a safe working environment, and prohibiting discrimination and harassment. Stay informed about changes in labor laws and update your policies and practices accordingly.

Environmental regulations aim to protect the environment and public health by regulating activities that impact air, water, and land. Depending on your industry, you may need to obtain environmental permits, conduct environmental assessments, and implement pollution control measures. Complying with environmental regulations not only helps you avoid legal penalties but also demonstrates your commitment to sustainability and corporate responsibility.

Consumer protection laws are designed to protect consumers from unfair, deceptive, or fraudulent business practices. These laws cover areas such as product safety, advertising, and privacy. Ensure that your products meet safety standards, provide clear and accurate information in your marketing materials, and protect customers' personal information. Implement policies and procedures to address customer complaints and resolve disputes fairly.

Industry-specific regulations vary depending on the nature of your business. For example, healthcare providers must comply with regulations governing patient privacy and medical licensing, while financial institutions must adhere to regulations related to banking and securities. Research the specific regulatory requirements for your industry and ensure that your business complies with all applicable laws.

Finally, it is important to establish clear and comprehensive contracts to protect your business interests and reduce the risk of disputes. Contracts are legally binding agreements that outline the rights and responsibilities of the parties involved. Common types of business contracts include partnership agreements, employment contracts, vendor agreements, and customer contracts. When drafting contracts, ensure that they are clear, specific, and enforceable. Include key terms such as payment terms, delivery schedules, confidentiality clauses, and dispute resolution mechanisms. Consider working with a contract attorney to review and draft your contracts to ensure that they meet legal requirements and protect your interests.

Establishing a solid legal foundation for your business involves choosing the right legal structure, registering your business, protecting your intellectual property, complying with regulations, and establishing clear contracts. By addressing these legal considerations early on, you can avoid potential legal issues, protect your business interests, and create a strong foundation for long-term success. Taking the time to build a comprehensive legal framework ensures that your business operates within the law and is well-positioned to thrive in a competitive market.

 කකක

"Brand identity is more than a logo; it's the essence of your business. It tells your story and connects with your audience. Build a brand that reflects your values and vision."

SIX

FUNDING YOUR VENTURE: EXPLORING FINANCING OPTIONS

Securing adequate funding is a pivotal aspect of launching and growing a business. Without sufficient capital, even the most promising ventures can falter. Exploring financing options requires a deep understanding of the available sources of funding, the requirements and implications of each, and a strategic approach to securing the necessary resources. Entrepreneurs must be well-prepared to navigate the complex landscape of business financing to ensure their venture has the financial foundation needed for success.

One of the primary sources of funding for new ventures is personal savings. Many entrepreneurs start by investing their own money into their business. This approach has several advantages, including full control over the business and no repayment obligations or interest costs. Using personal savings demonstrates a strong commitment to the venture, which can be appealing to potential investors and lenders.

However, this method also comes with significant risks, as the entrepreneur's personal financial security is directly tied to the success of the business. It is crucial to carefully assess the amount of personal savings that can be safely invested without jeopardizing personal financial stability.

Friends and family are another common source of initial funding. Loans or investments from friends and family can provide a quick and flexible source of capital. These individuals are often more willing to invest based on personal relationships and trust rather than formal business assessments.

However, mixing personal relationships with business can lead to complications if the business struggles or fails. Clear agreements and transparent communication are essential to managing these relationships and avoiding potential conflicts. It is advisable to formalize the terms of any loans or investments with written agreements outlining repayment terms, interest rates, and equity stakes.

Angel investors are individuals who provide capital to startups in exchange for equity ownership or convertible debt. They are often successful entrepreneurs or professionals who invest their own money and may also offer valuable mentorship and industry connections. Angel investors typically invest in the early stages of a business and are willing to take on higher risks for the potential of high returns. Finding angel investors requires networking and presenting a compelling business case.

Platforms such as AngelList and local angel investor networks can help entrepreneurs connect with potential investors. A well-prepared pitch that highlights the business's unique value proposition, market potential, and growth strategy is essential for attracting angel investment.

Venture capital (VC) is another significant source of funding, particularly for high-growth startups with substantial market potential. Venture capital firms pool funds from multiple investors to invest in promising businesses in exchange for equity. VC firms provide not only capital but also strategic guidance, industry expertise, and access to a network of resources.

The venture capital funding process is highly competitive, and securing VC investment requires a strong business plan, a scalable business model, and a proven track record of progress or traction. Entrepreneurs must be prepared for rigorous due diligence and negotiation processes. While venture capital can provide substantial funding and support, it also involves giving up a significant portion of equity and decision-making control.

Crowdfunding has emerged as a popular alternative financing option, leveraging the power of the internet and social media to raise funds from a large number of individuals. Platforms such as Kickstarter, Indiegogo, and GoFundMe allow entrepreneurs to pitch their business ideas to the public and solicit contributions. Crowdfunding can take various forms, including reward-based, equity-based, and donation-based models. Reward-based crowdfunding offers backers a product or service in return for their contributions, while equity-based crowdfunding provides backers with shares in the company.

Donation-based crowdfunding relies on contributions without any tangible return. Successful crowdfunding campaigns require a compelling story, a strong marketing strategy, and active engagement with backers. Crowdfunding not only provides funding but also serves as a marketing tool, helping to validate the business idea and build a community of early supporters.

Bank loans and lines of credit are traditional financing options for businesses. Banks offer various loan products, including term loans, equipment financing, and working capital loans, with fixed or variable interest rates. To qualify for a bank loan, entrepreneurs typically need a solid credit history, a detailed business plan, and collateral to secure the loan. The application process can be lengthy and requires extensive documentation.

While bank loans provide the advantage of retaining full ownership of the business, the repayment obligations and interest costs can be significant. Lines of credit offer more flexibility, allowing businesses to draw funds as needed and pay interest only on the amount borrowed. Establishing a good relationship with a bank and maintaining a strong credit profile are essential for accessing these financing options.

Small Business Administration (SBA) loans are another viable option for entrepreneurs in the United States. The SBA does not lend money directly but guarantees a portion of the loan, reducing the risk for lenders and making it easier for small businesses to obtain financing. SBA loan programs, such as the 7(a) Loan Program and the 504 Loan Program, offer competitive terms and lower down payments compared to traditional bank loans.

These loans can be used for various purposes, including working capital, equipment purchases, and real estate acquisition. The application process for SBA loans is rigorous, requiring detailed financial statements, business plans, and personal credit information. Working with an SBA-approved lender can help navigate the complexities of the application process.

Grants and competitions are sources of non-dilutive funding, meaning entrepreneurs do not have to give up equity or repay the funds. Grants are typically offered by government agencies, nonprofit organizations, and private foundations to support businesses that align with specific goals or initiatives, such as innovation, research and development, or social impact. Applying for grants involves a competitive process that requires a thorough understanding of the grantor's criteria and a well-crafted proposal.

Business competitions, such as pitch contests and startup accelerators, offer cash prizes, mentorship, and networking opportunities to winning participants. These competitions are an excellent way to gain exposure, validate the business idea, and attract additional investors.

Strategic partnerships and joint ventures can provide funding and valuable resources for business growth. Strategic partners may invest capital, share technology, provide access to distribution channels, or offer expertise in exchange for equity or revenue-sharing agreements.

Joint ventures involve two or more businesses collaborating on a specific project or business initiative, sharing resources, risks, and rewards. These arrangements can help businesses expand their market reach, enhance their capabilities, and accelerate growth. Identifying and negotiating with potential partners requires careful consideration of mutual goals, complementary strengths, and the terms of the partnership agreement.

Bootstrapping is the practice of self-funding a business using personal savings, revenue generated by the business, or minimal external funding. This approach requires a high level of financial discipline and resourcefulness. Bootstrapping allows entrepreneurs to retain full control and ownership of the business while avoiding debt and equity dilution. However, it also means limited access to capital, which can constrain growth and increase the time required to achieve business milestones. Successful bootstrapping often involves focusing on profitability from the outset, minimizing expenses, and reinvesting profits into the business.

Convertible notes and SAFE (Simple Agreement for Future Equity) agreements are financing instruments commonly used by startups to raise early-stage capital. Convertible notes are short-term debt instruments that convert into equity upon a future financing event, such as a venture capital round. They provide a way for investors to invest in a startup with the expectation of receiving equity in the future at a discounted rate. SAFE agreements, introduced by Y Combinator, are similar to convertible notes but do not accrue interest or have a maturity date. Both instruments offer flexibility and simplicity, allowing startups to raise funds quickly without the complexities of a traditional equity round.

Revenue-based financing is an alternative funding model where investors provide capital in exchange for a percentage of future revenue until a predetermined amount is repaid. This model aligns the interests of the investor and the business, as repayments are tied to the business's performance. Revenue-based financing can be particularly attractive for businesses with predictable and recurring revenue streams. The application process is typically faster and less stringent than traditional loans, but the cost of capital can be higher due to the variable repayment structure.

Peer-to-peer (P2P) lending platforms connect borrowers directly with individual lenders, offering an alternative to traditional bank loans. These platforms, such as LendingClub and Prosper, allow entrepreneurs to access funding from a broad network of investors. P2P lending can offer competitive interest rates and more flexible terms compared to traditional loans. The application process is typically streamlined, with faster approval times. However, borrowers must meet certain creditworthiness criteria, and the loan amounts may be limited compared to other financing options.

Trade credit and supplier financing are short-term financing options that allow businesses to purchase goods or services on credit from suppliers. This arrangement provides businesses with the flexibility to manage cash flow and maintain inventory without immediate payment. Trade credit terms vary, but typically involve payment within 30 to 90 days.

Supplier financing, also known as vendor financing, involves suppliers extending credit to customers to facilitate purchases. Establishing strong relationships with suppliers and demonstrating reliable payment history can help businesses negotiate favorable credit terms and enhance their financial flexibility.

Choosing the right financing option for your business depends on various factors, including the stage of your business, the amount of capital needed, the level of risk you are willing to assume, and your long-term goals. It is essential to carefully evaluate the pros and cons of each option and consider how they align with your business strategy. Diversifying your funding sources can help mitigate risks and provide a more stable financial foundation.

Preparing a comprehensive and compelling business plan is crucial for attracting investors and securing funding. Your business plan should clearly articulate your business concept, market opportunity, competitive advantage, revenue model, and financial projections. It should demonstrate your understanding of the market, your strategic vision, and your ability to execute your plan effectively. Investors and lenders look for well-thought-out plans that convey confidence, competence, and a realistic path to profitability.

Building relationships and networking are also critical components of the funding process. Attending industry events, joining business networks, and connecting with mentors and advisors can help you gain valuable insights, build credibility, and identify potential funding opportunities. Building a strong professional network can open doors to investors, partners, and customers, enhancing your business's prospects for success.

In summary, exploring financing options for your venture involves understanding the various sources of funding, evaluating their suitability for your business, and strategically securing the necessary capital. Whether through personal savings, loans, angel investors, venture capital, crowdfunding, or alternative financing models, each option has its advantages and challenges.

By carefully assessing your needs, preparing a robust business plan, and building strong relationships, you can navigate the complex landscape of business financing and lay a solid foundation for your venture's growth and success.

ᎮᎮᎮ

"A strong digital presence is crucial in today's market. It amplifies your reach and engages your audience. Embrace the digital age to thrive and grow."

SEVEN

Brand Identity: Creating a Memorable Brand

Creating a memorable brand identity is a crucial aspect of building a successful business. A strong brand identity helps differentiate your business from competitors, establishes a unique presence in the market, and fosters customer loyalty. It encompasses the visual, emotional, and cultural elements that communicate what your business stands for and what it promises to deliver. Developing a compelling brand identity involves understanding your target audience, defining your brand's core values and mission, creating a cohesive visual identity, and consistently communicating your brand message across all touchpoints.

The first step in creating a memorable brand identity is to understand your target audience. Knowing who your customers are, what they need, and what motivates them is essential for developing a brand that resonates with them. Conduct thorough market research to gather insights about your audience's demographics, psychographics, and behavior.

Demographic information includes age, gender, income, education, and location, while psychographic details encompass lifestyle, values, interests, and attitudes. Understanding your audience's behavior involves analyzing their purchasing habits, brand preferences, and decision-making processes. By gaining a deep understanding of your target audience, you can create a brand identity that speaks directly to their needs and desires.

Once you have a clear understanding of your target audience, the next step is to define your brand's core values and mission. Your core values are the guiding principles that shape your business's culture, decision-making, and interactions with customers. They reflect what your business stands for and what it believes in. Your mission statement, on the other hand, articulates your business's purpose and what it aims to achieve. It provides a clear and concise description of your business's goals and the value it offers to customers. Defining your core values and mission is essential for creating a brand identity that is authentic, consistent, and meaningful.

Creating a cohesive visual identity is a critical aspect of brand identity. Your visual identity includes elements such as your logo, color palette, typography, imagery, and design style. These elements work together to create a recognizable and consistent look and feel for your brand. Your logo is the most prominent visual representation of your brand and serves as a symbol of your business. It should be simple, memorable, and reflective of your brand's personality and values.

Your color palette should consist of a set of colors that convey the mood and tone of your brand. Colors have psychological associations and can evoke specific emotions, so choose colors that align with your brand's message and resonate with your audience.

Typography is another important element of your visual identity.

The fonts you choose should be legible and reflect the personality of your brand. For example, a modern and innovative brand might choose sleek, sans-serif fonts, while a traditional and elegant brand might opt for classic serif fonts. Consistent use of typography across all brand materials helps create a cohesive and professional appearance.

Imagery, including photos, illustrations, and graphics, plays a significant role in conveying your brand's story and values. Select imagery that aligns with your brand's aesthetic and resonates with your audience. Your design style, which encompasses the overall look and feel of your brand materials, should be consistent across all touchpoints, from your website and social media profiles to your packaging and marketing materials.

Consistency is key to building a strong brand identity. Your brand message, visual identity, and customer experience should be consistent across all channels and touchpoints. Consistency helps build brand recognition and trust, as customers come to know what to expect from your brand. Develop brand guidelines that outline the rules for using your logo, color palette, typography, imagery, and tone of voice. These guidelines serve as a reference for anyone creating brand materials, ensuring that your brand is presented consistently and professionally.

Your brand message is the narrative that communicates who you are, what you do, and why it matters to your audience. It encompasses your value proposition, key messages, and brand story. Your value proposition is the unique benefit or advantage that your brand offers to customers.

It explains why customers should choose your brand over competitors and what sets you apart. Your key messages are the main points you want to communicate about your brand, such as your core values, mission, and benefits. Your brand story is the narrative that connects your brand to your audience on an emotional level. It explains the history, purpose, and vision of your brand, creating a sense of authenticity and relatability.

Communicating your brand message effectively involves using a consistent tone of voice and language that reflects your brand's personality and values. Your tone of voice should be tailored to your audience and the context in which you are communicating. For example, a tech startup might use an informal, conversational tone to appeal to a younger audience, while a financial services company might use a more formal and authoritative tone to convey trust and expertise.

Use language that resonates with your audience and reinforces your brand's message. Whether through social media posts, website copy, or customer service interactions, ensure that your brand's voice is consistent and aligned with your brand identity.

Engaging with your audience is an essential part of building a memorable brand identity. Building strong relationships with customers involves creating meaningful interactions and delivering exceptional experiences. Social media platforms provide an opportunity to connect with your audience, share your brand story, and engage in conversations.

Use social media to showcase your brand's personality, share valuable content, and respond to customer feedback. Encourage user-generated content, such as reviews, testimonials, and photos, to build a sense of community and trust around your brand.

Customer experience is a critical component of brand identity. Every interaction customers have with your brand, whether online or offline, contributes to their overall perception of your brand. Focus on delivering a seamless and positive customer experience at every touchpoint. This includes providing excellent customer service, ensuring a user-friendly website, and creating a memorable unboxing experience for your products.

Pay attention to the details that enhance the customer journey and exceed their expectations. A positive customer experience fosters loyalty and advocacy, as satisfied customers are more likely to recommend your brand to others.

Storytelling is a powerful tool for creating a memorable brand identity. Humans are naturally drawn to stories, and a compelling brand story can create an emotional connection with your audience. Your brand story should be authentic, relatable, and aligned with your core values and mission. Share the journey of your brand, including the challenges and triumphs, to create a sense of authenticity and transparency. Highlight the people behind your brand, including the founders, employees, and customers, to humanize your brand and build relatability. Use storytelling to convey your brand's purpose, vision, and the impact you aim to make in the world.

Building brand loyalty involves consistently delivering on your brand promise and maintaining a strong relationship with your customers. Loyalty programs, personalized experiences, and exclusive offers can help foster loyalty and reward repeat customers. Show appreciation for your customers through gestures such as thank-you notes, special discounts, and personalized messages. Collect and act on customer feedback to continuously improve your products, services, and customer experience. By showing that you value and care about your customers, you can build long-lasting relationships and turn customers into brand advocates.

Adapting your brand identity to changing market conditions and customer preferences is essential for long-term success. While consistency is important, it is also necessary to evolve and stay relevant. Monitor market trends, competitor activities, and customer feedback to identify opportunities for innovation and improvement. Be open to refining your brand identity and messaging to better align with the evolving needs of your audience. However, ensure that any changes remain true to your core values and mission, maintaining the authenticity and integrity of your brand.

Collaborations and partnerships can enhance your brand identity and expand your reach. Partnering with complementary brands, influencers, or industry leaders can introduce your brand to new audiences and create synergies. Collaborations should be strategically aligned with your brand values and goals, and both parties should benefit from the partnership. Joint marketing campaigns, co-branded products, and influencer endorsements can increase brand visibility and credibility.

Measuring the effectiveness of your brand identity is essential for understanding its impact and making informed decisions. Use metrics such as brand awareness, brand recall, customer satisfaction, and loyalty to assess the strength of your brand identity. Conduct surveys, focus groups, and social media analysis to gather qualitative insights about customer perceptions and experiences.

Monitor key performance indicators (KPIs) related to marketing campaigns, website traffic, and sales to evaluate the success of your branding efforts. Use the insights gained from these assessments to refine your brand strategy and enhance your brand identity.

Building a memorable brand identity is an ongoing process that requires dedication, creativity, and strategic thinking. It involves understanding your target audience, defining your brand's core values and mission, creating a cohesive visual identity, and consistently communicating your brand message. Engaging with your audience, delivering exceptional customer experiences, and using storytelling to create emotional connections are essential components of a strong brand identity.

By maintaining consistency, adapting to changing conditions, and measuring the impact of your branding efforts, you can build a memorable and successful brand that resonates with your audience and stands out in the market. A strong brand identity not only attracts customers but also fosters loyalty and advocacy, contributing to the long-term success of your business.

❦❦❦

"Product development is the heart of entrepreneurship. It brings ideas to life and meets customer needs. Innovate continuously to stay relevant and competitive."

EIGHT

DIGITAL PRESENCE: ESTABLISHING YOUR ONLINE FOOTPRINT

Establishing a robust digital presence is essential for modern businesses aiming to reach and engage with their target audience. As the digital landscape continues to evolve, businesses must adapt and leverage online platforms to enhance their visibility, credibility, and accessibility. Creating a comprehensive online footprint involves developing a professional website, engaging on social media, optimizing for search engines, and utilizing digital marketing strategies to connect with customers and drive growth.

A professional website serves as the cornerstone of your digital presence. It is often the first point of contact between your business and potential customers, making it crucial to create a website that is visually appealing, user-friendly, and informative. Start by choosing a clean and responsive design that works seamlessly across various devices, including desktops, tablets, and smartphones. The design should reflect your brand identity, using consistent colors, fonts, and imagery to create a cohesive look and feel.

Content is a critical component of your website, as it provides valuable information to visitors and helps establish your authority in your industry. Develop high-quality content that addresses the needs and interests of your target audience. This includes detailed product or service descriptions, informative blog posts, customer testimonials, case studies, and frequently asked questions (FAQs). Use clear and concise language, and incorporate keywords relevant to your industry to improve search engine optimization (SEO).

SEO is essential for increasing your website's visibility on search engines like Google. By optimizing your website for SEO, you can improve your search rankings and attract more organic traffic. This involves conducting keyword research to identify the terms and phrases your target audience is searching for and incorporating these keywords into your website content, meta tags, and URLs. Additionally, ensure that your website is technically optimized, with fast loading times, secure connections (HTTPS), and mobile-friendly design. Building high-quality backlinks from reputable websites can also enhance your SEO efforts and boost your search rankings.

Social media is another vital component of your digital presence. It provides a platform to engage with your audience, build relationships, and promote your brand. Start by identifying the social media platforms most relevant to your business and target audience, such as Facebook, Instagram, Twitter, LinkedIn, and Pinterest. Each platform has its unique features and audience, so tailor your content and strategy accordingly.

Creating engaging and shareable content is key to building a strong social media presence. This includes a mix of promotional posts, educational content, behind-the-scenes glimpses, user-generated content, and interactive posts like polls and quizzes. Use high-quality images and videos to capture your audience's attention and convey your brand message effectively. Consistency is crucial, so develop a content calendar to plan and schedule your posts regularly.

Social media also offers opportunities for paid advertising, allowing you to reach a larger and more targeted audience. Platforms like Facebook and Instagram offer sophisticated ad targeting options based on demographics, interests, behaviors, and location. Develop compelling ad creatives and copy that resonate with your target audience, and use analytics to track the performance of your ads and optimize your campaigns for better results.

Email marketing is another powerful tool for establishing your digital presence and nurturing relationships with your audience. Building an email list allows you to communicate directly with your customers and prospects, providing valuable content, promotions, and updates. Start by creating lead magnets, such as ebooks, whitepapers, or exclusive discounts, to encourage visitors to subscribe to your email list. Use email marketing platforms like Mailchimp, Constant Contact, or HubSpot to design and send professional-looking emails.

Segment your email list based on factors like customer behavior, preferences, and purchase history to deliver personalized and relevant content. Develop automated email sequences to engage with subscribers at different stages of the customer journey, such as welcome emails, abandoned cart reminders, and post-purchase follow-ups. Regularly analyze your email marketing metrics, such as open rates, click-through rates, and conversions, to refine your strategy and improve your results.

Content marketing is a crucial aspect of your digital presence, helping you attract, engage, and retain your audience by providing valuable and relevant content. This includes blog posts, articles, videos, podcasts, infographics, and webinars. Develop a content strategy that aligns with your business goals and addresses the needs and interests of your target audience. Use storytelling to make your content more engaging and relatable, and incorporate keywords to improve SEO.

Guest blogging and collaborations with influencers or industry experts can also enhance your content marketing efforts. By contributing to reputable websites and partnering with influential figures, you can expand your reach, build credibility, and attract new audiences to your brand. Repurpose your content across different formats and platforms to maximize its impact and reach a wider audience.

Online reviews and reputation management are critical for building trust and credibility in the digital space. Encourage satisfied customers to leave positive reviews on platforms like Google My Business, Yelp, and industry-specific review sites. Respond promptly and professionally to both positive and negative reviews, demonstrating your commitment to customer satisfaction. Addressing negative feedback constructively can help resolve issues and improve your reputation.

Pay-per-click (PPC) advertising is another effective way to establish your digital presence and drive traffic to your website. Platforms like Google Ads and Bing Ads allow you to create targeted ads that appear at the top of search engine results pages (SERPs) for specific keywords. Develop compelling ad copy and use relevant keywords to attract clicks from potential customers. Use PPC campaigns to promote special offers, new products, or specific landing pages on your website. Monitor your ad performance regularly and adjust your bids, keywords, and ad copy to optimize your campaigns and maximize your return on investment (ROI).

Analytics and data-driven decision-making are essential for measuring the effectiveness of your digital presence and making informed improvements. Use tools like Google Analytics, social media insights, and email marketing analytics to track key performance indicators (KPIs) such as website traffic, engagement, conversions, and revenue. Analyze the data to identify trends, strengths, and areas for improvement. Use these insights to refine your digital strategy, optimize your campaigns, and achieve better results.

Local SEO is crucial for businesses that rely on local customers, such as brick-and-mortar stores or service providers. Optimize your website and online listings for local search by including location-specific keywords, creating a Google My Business profile, and ensuring consistent and accurate information across all online directories. Encourage satisfied customers to leave positive reviews on your Google My Business profile, and engage with the local community through events, sponsorships, and partnerships.

Video marketing is an increasingly important aspect of digital presence, with platforms like YouTube, Facebook, and Instagram offering powerful opportunities to reach and engage your audience. Create high-quality videos that showcase your products, tell your brand story, provide tutorials, or share customer testimonials. Use live streaming to connect with your audience in real-time, answer questions, and provide exclusive content. Optimize your videos for SEO by including relevant keywords in the titles, descriptions, and tags, and encourage viewers to like, comment, and share your videos.

Building a strong digital presence requires a strategic and integrated approach, combining various online platforms and marketing techniques to create a cohesive and effective online footprint. It is essential to stay updated with the latest digital trends, tools, and best practices to remain competitive and relevant in the ever-evolving digital landscape. Continuously evaluate and adjust your digital strategy based on performance data, industry trends, and customer feedback to achieve sustainable growth and success.

In conclusion, establishing a robust digital presence involves creating a professional website, engaging on social media, optimizing for search engines, leveraging email marketing, and utilizing content marketing strategies. Additionally, managing online reviews, utilizing PPC advertising, and employing data-driven decision-making are essential for building and maintaining a strong online footprint. By adopting a strategic and integrated approach to digital presence, businesses can enhance their visibility, credibility, and accessibility, ultimately driving growth and success in the digital age.

ᐳᐳᐳ

"Pricing strategies are an art and science. Balance affordability with profitability. Understand your market to set prices that attract and retain customers."

NINE

PRODUCT DEVELOPMENT: BRINGING YOUR IDEA TO LIFE

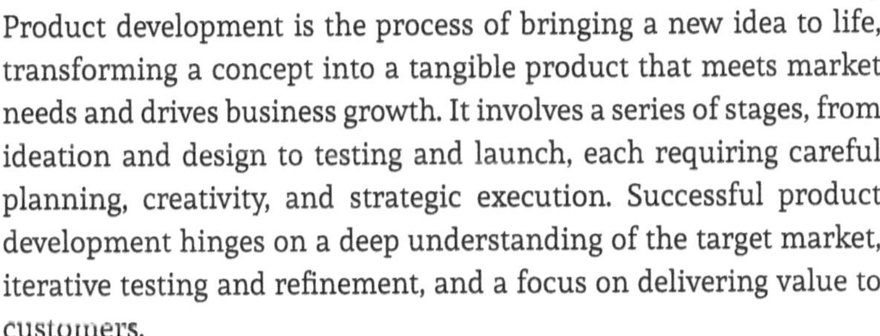

Product development is the process of bringing a new idea to life, transforming a concept into a tangible product that meets market needs and drives business growth. It involves a series of stages, from ideation and design to testing and launch, each requiring careful planning, creativity, and strategic execution. Successful product development hinges on a deep understanding of the target market, iterative testing and refinement, and a focus on delivering value to customers.

The journey begins with ideation, where the initial concept for the product is conceived. This stage is marked by creativity and brainstorming, as ideas are generated, discussed, and refined. Ideation can be sparked by identifying a gap in the market, solving a problem, or improving upon existing products. It often involves input from diverse sources, including customers, employees, industry experts, and market trends. Techniques such as mind mapping, brainstorming sessions, and SWOT analysis (Strengths, Weaknesses, Opportunities, Threats) can facilitate the generation of innovative ideas.

Once a promising idea has been identified, the next step is to conduct thorough market research to validate its potential. Market research involves gathering data on the target audience, competitors, and industry trends. Understanding the needs, preferences, and pain points of the target market is crucial for developing a product that resonates with customers. This research can be conducted through surveys, interviews, focus groups, and analysis of existing market data. Competitor analysis helps identify what similar products are available, their strengths and weaknesses, and areas where your product can differentiate itself. Market research provides the foundation for informed decision-making and reduces the risk of product failure.

With a validated idea and a clear understanding of the market, the next phase is to define the product requirements. This involves outlining the features, functionalities, and specifications of the product. A detailed product requirements document serves as a blueprint for the development process, ensuring that all stakeholders have a clear understanding of what the product will entail. It should include technical specifications, design requirements, performance criteria, and any regulatory or compliance considerations. Collaborating with cross-functional teams, such as engineering, design, marketing, and sales, is essential to ensure that the product requirements align with business goals and customer needs.

Design is a critical stage in product development, where the conceptual idea takes a tangible form. This phase involves creating detailed designs, prototypes, and mock-ups of the product. The design process should prioritize usability, functionality, and aesthetics, ensuring that the product not only meets technical specifications but also provides a positive user experience. Prototyping is an iterative process that allows for the testing and refinement of design concepts. Initial prototypes can be simple and low-cost, serving as a proof of concept. As the design progresses, more advanced and functional prototypes are developed to test specific features and functionalities.

Testing and validation are integral components of the product development process. Rigorous testing helps identify and address any issues or defects before the product is launched to the market. This stage involves various types of testing, including functional testing, usability testing, performance testing, and user acceptance testing. Functional testing ensures that the product operates as intended and meets the defined specifications. Usability testing assesses the user experience, evaluating how easy and intuitive the product is to use. Performance testing measures the product's efficiency, reliability, and scalability under different conditions. User acceptance testing involves real users interacting with the product to provide feedback and validate its effectiveness.

Iterative testing and feedback loops are essential for refining the product and ensuring its success. Feedback from users and stakeholders should be collected, analyzed, and incorporated into the design and development process. This iterative approach allows for continuous improvement and ensures that the final product aligns with customer expectations and market demands. Agile methodologies, such as Scrum or Kanban, can facilitate iterative development and promote collaboration among cross-functional teams.

Once the product has been thoroughly tested and refined, it is ready for production and launch. The production phase involves manufacturing the product at scale, ensuring that it meets quality standards and regulatory requirements. This stage requires careful planning and coordination with suppliers, manufacturers, and logistics providers to ensure a smooth and efficient production process. Quality control measures should be implemented to monitor and maintain product quality throughout the production cycle.

The launch phase is a critical milestone in the product development process, marking the introduction of the product to the market. A successful product launch requires a well-executed marketing and sales strategy to generate awareness, interest, and demand. This involves creating a compelling value proposition, developing marketing materials, and executing promotional campaigns across various channels. Leveraging digital marketing, social media, public relations, and influencer partnerships can help amplify the reach and impact of the product launch. Engaging with early adopters and gathering feedback post-launch is essential for identifying any issues and making necessary adjustments.

Post-launch, it is important to monitor the product's performance and gather data on customer satisfaction, sales, and market reception. This data provides valuable insights into the product's success and areas for improvement. Customer feedback should be continuously collected and analyzed to identify trends, preferences, and pain points. Regular updates and enhancements based on customer feedback can help maintain the product's relevance and competitiveness in the market.

Product development is not a one-time event but an ongoing process of innovation and improvement. Staying attuned to market trends, emerging technologies, and customer needs is essential for sustaining long-term success. Continuous innovation involves exploring new features, functionalities, and use cases for the product, as well as identifying opportunities for new product development. Building a culture of innovation within the organization, encouraging experimentation, and fostering collaboration are key factors in driving continuous product development.

Collaboration and communication are critical throughout the product development process. Effective collaboration among cross-functional teams, including engineering, design, marketing, sales, and customer support, ensures that all aspects of the product are aligned and integrated. Clear and transparent communication helps manage expectations, resolve conflicts, and keep the project on track. Regular meetings, progress updates, and collaborative tools can facilitate communication and coordination among team members.

Risk management is another important aspect of product development. Identifying and mitigating potential risks, such as technical challenges, market uncertainties, and regulatory compliance, is essential for minimizing disruptions and ensuring a successful outcome. Conducting a risk assessment and developing contingency plans can help address potential issues proactively. Engaging with legal and regulatory experts can ensure that the product complies with relevant laws and standards.

Budget and resource management are critical factors in the success of product development. Allocating sufficient resources, including time, budget, and personnel, is essential for achieving project goals and milestones. Effective project management involves setting realistic timelines, managing costs, and ensuring that resources are utilized efficiently. Tracking progress and adjusting plans as needed can help keep the project on schedule and within budget.

Building strong relationships with suppliers, manufacturers, and partners is essential for a successful product development process. Collaborating with reliable and experienced partners can help streamline production, ensure quality, and reduce lead times. Negotiating favorable terms and maintaining open communication with suppliers and manufacturers can enhance the efficiency and effectiveness of the production process.

Intellectual property protection is an important consideration in product development. Securing patents, trademarks, and copyrights can protect the product's unique features, design, and branding from infringement. Working with intellectual property experts can help navigate the complexities of IP protection and ensure that the product's innovations are safeguarded.

In conclusion, product development is a multifaceted process that involves bringing a new idea to life through ideation, market research, design, testing, production, and launch. It requires careful planning, creativity, and strategic execution, as well as a deep understanding of the target market and a focus on delivering value to customers. Iterative testing, feedback loops, and continuous improvement are essential for refining the product and ensuring its success. Collaboration, communication, risk management, and resource management are critical factors in achieving project goals and sustaining long-term success. By following a structured and strategic approach to product development, businesses can create innovative products that meet market needs and drive growth.

❧❧❧

"Marketing is the bridge between your product and your customers. Use it to build relationships and drive engagement. Effective marketing turns prospects into loyal customers."

TEN

PRICING STRATEGIES: SETTING COMPETITIVE AND PROFITABLE PRICES

Setting competitive and profitable prices is a crucial aspect of any business strategy. Pricing strategies not only influence revenue and profitability but also affect brand perception, market positioning, and customer behavior. Effective pricing requires a deep understanding of costs, market demand, competition, and perceived value. A well-crafted pricing strategy aligns with business goals, captures value for customers, and ensures long-term sustainability.

At the core of any pricing strategy is the need to cover costs and generate profit. This involves understanding both fixed and variable costs associated with producing and delivering a product or service. Fixed costs, such as rent, salaries, and utilities, remain constant regardless of the number of units sold. Variable costs, such as raw materials, packaging, and shipping, fluctuate with production volume. By calculating the total cost of goods sold (COGS), businesses can determine the minimum price required to break even. However, simply covering costs is not sufficient; pricing must also reflect the value delivered to customers and the competitive landscape.

Market demand plays a pivotal role in determining pricing. Demand-based pricing, also known as dynamic pricing, involves setting prices based on the perceived value to the customer and their willingness to pay. This approach requires thorough market research to understand customer preferences, price sensitivity, and purchasing behavior. Tools such as surveys, focus groups, and A/B testing can provide insights into how different price points affect demand. Price elasticity of demand measures the responsiveness of quantity demanded to changes in price. Products with inelastic demand see little change in quantity sold with price fluctuations, while products with elastic demand experience significant changes. Understanding elasticity helps businesses set prices that maximize revenue without negatively impacting sales volume.

Competitive analysis is another critical component of pricing strategy. Competitor-based pricing involves setting prices relative to competitors' offerings. This approach requires a comprehensive understanding of the competitive landscape, including the prices, features, and market positions of similar products. Businesses can choose to price their products higher, lower, or at parity with competitors based on their value proposition and market positioning. Premium pricing, or skimming, involves setting higher prices to signal superior quality or exclusivity. This strategy is effective for luxury brands or innovative products with unique features. Conversely, penetration pricing involves setting lower prices to quickly gain market share and attract price-sensitive customers. This strategy is often used by new entrants or businesses aiming to disrupt established markets.

Value-based pricing focuses on setting prices based on the perceived value to the customer rather than solely on costs or competition. This strategy requires a deep understanding of customer needs, preferences, and the benefits they derive from the product. By emphasizing the unique value proposition and differentiating features, businesses can justify higher prices and enhance customer loyalty. Communicating the value effectively through marketing and customer education is essential for this strategy to succeed. For example, a software company might highlight time savings, efficiency improvements, or cost reductions achieved by using their product.

Psychological pricing leverages cognitive biases and perceptions to influence purchasing decisions. Techniques such as charm pricing, where prices end in .99 or .95, create the perception of a lower cost. For instance, pricing a product at $9.99 instead of $10 can make it seem significantly cheaper. Anchoring involves presenting a higher-priced option alongside the target product to make it appear more affordable. Bundling offers multiple products or services together at a discounted price, creating the perception of added value. Price framing, where discounts are presented as savings rather than reduced prices, also enhances perceived value. Understanding psychological principles helps businesses craft pricing strategies that appeal to customer behavior and perceptions.

Dynamic pricing, enabled by advanced analytics and technology, allows businesses to adjust prices in real-time based on various factors such as demand, competition, inventory levels, and customer segments. This approach is commonly used in industries like travel, hospitality, and e-commerce. Algorithms analyze data and optimize prices to maximize revenue and profitability. Surge pricing, used by ride-sharing companies, increases prices during peak demand periods to balance supply and demand. While dynamic pricing can enhance profitability, it requires sophisticated systems and careful management to avoid customer backlash and ensure fairness.

Promotional pricing involves temporarily reducing prices to stimulate sales and attract customers. Techniques such as discounts, coupons, seasonal sales, and limited-time offers create urgency and incentivize purchases. While promotional pricing can boost short-term sales and clear excess inventory, it must be used strategically to avoid eroding brand value and long-term profitability. Frequent discounts can condition customers to expect lower prices and undermine the perceived value of the product. Balancing promotional activities with maintaining a strong brand image is crucial for sustaining long-term growth.

Subscription-based pricing models offer customers access to products or services for a recurring fee, typically monthly or annually. This approach provides a predictable revenue stream and fosters customer loyalty. Subscription models are prevalent in industries such as software (SaaS), media, and consumer goods. Businesses can offer tiered pricing plans with different levels of features or benefits to cater to diverse customer needs. Freemium models provide basic services for free while charging for premium features. Successful subscription models require delivering consistent value, engaging customers, and minimizing churn through excellent service and continuous innovation.

Geographical pricing considers regional differences in costs, demand, and competitive dynamics. Businesses may set different prices for the same product in various locations based on factors such as cost of living, local competition, and market conditions. This approach allows businesses to optimize pricing for different markets and maximize profitability. Implementing geographical pricing requires careful analysis of regional market data and an understanding of local customer preferences and behavior.

Price segmentation involves charging different prices to different customer segments based on their willingness to pay. This strategy can be implemented through various means, such as customer loyalty programs, volume discounts, student or senior pricing, and early-bird discounts. Price segmentation allows businesses to capture more value from different customer groups and enhance overall profitability. It requires a robust understanding of customer segments and effective communication to avoid perceptions of unfairness or discrimination.

Cost-plus pricing, or markup pricing, involves adding a fixed percentage to the cost of goods sold to determine the selling price. This straightforward approach ensures that costs are covered and a consistent profit margin is maintained. However, it may not fully account for market demand, competition, or perceived value. While cost-plus pricing provides simplicity and predictability, it should be supplemented with other pricing strategies to ensure competitiveness and responsiveness to market conditions.

Life-cycle pricing recognizes that products go through different stages—introduction, growth, maturity, and decline—and pricing strategies should evolve accordingly. During the introduction phase, businesses may use penetration pricing to attract early adopters or skimming to maximize initial profits. As the product gains traction and enters the growth phase, prices can be adjusted to capture a broader market. In the maturity phase, competitive pressures may necessitate price reductions or added value through enhancements. During the decline phase, businesses may use clearance pricing to liquidate inventory. Adapting pricing strategies to the product life cycle helps optimize revenue and manage market transitions effectively.

International pricing involves setting prices for products sold in different countries, considering factors such as currency exchange rates, local purchasing power, taxes, and import duties. Global pricing strategies may include standardization, where the same price is set worldwide, or adaptation, where prices are adjusted based on local conditions. Factors such as economic stability, competitive landscape, and cultural differences influence international pricing decisions. Managing international pricing requires a deep understanding of global markets and coordination with local partners to ensure compliance and competitiveness.

Implementing an effective pricing strategy requires continuous monitoring and analysis. Businesses should regularly review pricing performance, customer feedback, and market conditions to make data-driven adjustments. Price testing, such as A/B testing different price points, provides valuable insights into customer preferences and price elasticity. Advanced analytics and machine learning can enhance pricing optimization by identifying patterns and predicting demand. Flexibility and agility in pricing decisions enable businesses to respond to market changes and seize opportunities.

Communicating pricing effectively is essential for customer acceptance and satisfaction. Transparent pricing builds trust and reduces confusion or frustration. Clearly explain the value proposition, the benefits included in the price, and any additional costs or terms. Use pricing psychology to frame prices positively and highlight savings or value. Consistent communication across all channels—website, marketing materials, customer service—ensures a cohesive and clear pricing message.

Ethical considerations in pricing are increasingly important in building long-term customer trust and brand reputation. Practices such as price gouging, deceptive pricing, and unfair discrimination can harm customer relationships and attract regulatory scrutiny. Ethical pricing involves fairness, transparency, and respect for customer value. Businesses should consider the broader impact of their pricing decisions on customers, communities, and society. Balancing profitability with ethical principles fosters sustainable growth and positive brand perception.

In conclusion, setting competitive and profitable prices requires a strategic approach that considers costs, market demand, competition, perceived value, and psychological factors. Effective pricing strategies align with business goals, capture value for customers, and ensure long-term sustainability. By understanding and leveraging various pricing techniques—demand-based, competitor-based, value-based, psychological, dynamic, promotional, subscription-based, geographical, segmented, cost-plus, life-cycle, and international pricing—businesses can optimize revenue and profitability. Continuous monitoring, analysis, and ethical considerations are essential for adapting pricing strategies to evolving market conditions and maintaining customer trust. A well-executed pricing strategy is a powerful tool for driving business success and achieving competitive advantage.

ppp

"Sales techniques are about understanding and connecting with customers. Build trust and offer solutions. Successful sales are built on strong relationships."

ELEVEN

Marketing Tactics: Reaching and Engaging Your Target Market

Effective marketing tactics are essential for reaching and engaging your target market, driving customer acquisition, and building brand loyalty. The modern marketing landscape is dynamic and multifaceted, requiring businesses to adopt a mix of strategies that leverage both digital and traditional channels. Understanding your target audience, crafting compelling messages, and utilizing various platforms to reach them are crucial steps in developing a successful marketing plan.

The foundation of any marketing strategy is a deep understanding of your target market. This involves identifying who your customers are, what they need, and how they behave. Demographic information such as age, gender, income, education, and location provides a basic profile of your audience. Psychographic details, including values, interests, lifestyles, and attitudes, offer deeper insights into what motivates your customers. Behavioral data, such as purchasing patterns, brand loyalty, and online activity, helps predict future actions and tailor marketing efforts accordingly. Collecting and analyzing this information through market research, surveys, and customer data platforms enables businesses to create detailed customer personas that guide marketing decisions.

Once you have a clear picture of your target market, the next step is to craft compelling messages that resonate with them. Effective messaging highlights the unique value proposition of your product or service, addressing the specific needs and pain points of your audience. It should be clear, concise, and consistent across all marketing channels. Storytelling is a powerful tool in crafting engaging messages, as it creates an emotional connection with the audience. By sharing the story behind your brand, the journey of your products, and the impact on customers' lives, you can build authenticity and trust. Tailoring your messages to different segments of your audience ensures relevance and increases the likelihood of engagement.

Digital marketing has become a cornerstone of modern marketing tactics due to its reach, cost-effectiveness, and ability to target specific audiences. Search engine optimization (SEO) is critical for improving the visibility of your website on search engines like Google. By optimizing your site's content, structure, and technical elements for relevant keywords, you can attract organic traffic from users actively searching for products or services like yours. Content marketing, including blog posts, articles, videos, and infographics, provides valuable information to your audience, establishing your brand as an authority in your industry and driving traffic to your site.

Social media marketing leverages platforms like Facebook,

Instagram, Twitter, LinkedIn, and Pinterest to engage with your audience, build relationships, and promote your brand. Each platform has its unique features and user demographics, so it is essential to tailor your content and strategy accordingly. Visual content, such as images and videos, tends to perform well on social media, capturing attention and encouraging sharing. Interactive content, such as polls, quizzes, and live videos, fosters engagement and provides real-time feedback. Paid social media advertising allows for precise targeting based on demographics, interests, and behaviors, maximizing the reach and effectiveness of your campaigns.

Email marketing remains one of the most effective tactics for nurturing leads and maintaining customer relationships. Building an email list involves offering valuable content or incentives in exchange for contact information. Segmentation allows for personalized communication, ensuring that the right messages reach the right audience at the right time. Automated email sequences, such as welcome series, abandoned cart reminders, and post-purchase follow-ups, enhance the customer journey and drive conversions. Regular newsletters keep your audience informed about new products, promotions, and company news. Monitoring metrics like open rates, click-through rates, and conversion rates helps optimize email campaigns for better performance.

Pay-per-click (PPC) advertising, particularly through platforms like Google Ads, enables businesses to place ads in front of users searching for specific keywords. PPC campaigns can drive immediate traffic to your website and generate leads quickly. Effective PPC advertising requires thorough keyword research, compelling ad copy, and optimized landing pages. Retargeting campaigns, which show ads to users who have previously visited your site, can remind potential customers of your brand and encourage them to complete their purchase. Monitoring and adjusting bids, keywords, and ad placements ensures that your PPC campaigns remain cost-effective and yield a high return on investment (ROI).

Influencer marketing leverages the reach and credibility of individuals with large followings on social media or other platforms. By partnering with influencers whose audiences align with your target market, you can increase brand awareness and drive engagement. Influencers can create authentic content that showcases your products, share their experiences, and recommend your brand to their followers. Micro-influencers, who have smaller but highly engaged audiences, can be particularly effective for niche markets. Establishing clear goals, selecting the right influencers, and measuring the impact of influencer campaigns are essential for success.

Content marketing goes beyond blog posts and articles to include a variety of formats such as videos, podcasts, webinars, and ebooks. Videos, in particular, are highly engaging and can convey complex information in an easily digestible format. Creating a mix of educational, entertaining, and promotional content keeps your audience engaged and builds trust in your brand. Webinars and live events provide opportunities for direct interaction with your audience, allowing you to showcase your expertise, answer questions, and gather feedback. Offering free resources like ebooks or whitepapers in exchange for contact information can help generate leads and expand your email list.

Search engine marketing (SEM) combines SEO and PPC tactics to maximize visibility on search engines. While SEO focuses on organic search results, SEM includes paid search advertising to ensure your brand appears at the top of search results for targeted keywords. A balanced SEM strategy drives traffic from both organic and paid sources, enhancing overall online presence. Regularly updating and optimizing your website content, monitoring keyword performance, and adjusting ad campaigns based on analytics are crucial for maintaining a strong search engine presence.

Traditional marketing tactics, such as print advertising, direct mail, radio, and television, still play a role in reaching certain segments of the market. These channels can complement digital efforts by providing additional touchpoints and reinforcing brand messages. Direct mail, for example, can be highly targeted and personalized, making it an effective way to reach specific audiences. Combining traditional and digital marketing tactics through integrated campaigns creates a cohesive and comprehensive marketing strategy.

Event marketing, including trade shows, conferences, and product launches, offers opportunities for face-to-face interaction with potential customers and industry peers. Events allow you to showcase your products, network with other businesses, and gather valuable market insights. Hosting or sponsoring events can enhance brand visibility and credibility. Virtual events and webinars have gained popularity as cost-effective alternatives that can reach a global audience without the logistical challenges of physical events.

Public relations (PR) focuses on building and maintaining a positive image for your brand through media coverage, press releases, and community engagement. Effective PR strategies generate buzz and enhance credibility by securing coverage in reputable publications and media outlets. Building relationships with journalists and industry influencers, crafting compelling press releases, and participating in community initiatives can elevate your brand's reputation and visibility.

Customer advocacy and referral programs leverage the power of satisfied customers to promote your brand. Encouraging customers to share their positive experiences and refer others can drive word-of-mouth marketing, which is highly influential. Offering incentives, such as discounts, rewards, or exclusive access, motivates customers to participate in referral programs. Collecting and showcasing customer testimonials and reviews on your website and social media adds authenticity and builds trust.

Analytics and data-driven decision-making are essential for measuring the effectiveness of marketing tactics and making informed adjustments. Utilizing tools like Google Analytics, social media insights, email marketing analytics, and CRM systems provides valuable data on customer behavior, campaign performance, and ROI. Regularly analyzing this data helps identify trends, strengths, and areas for improvement. A/B testing different elements of your campaigns, such as headlines, images, and calls-to-action, provides insights into what resonates best with your audience.

Agility and adaptability are crucial in the ever-evolving marketing landscape. Staying updated with the latest trends, technologies, and best practices enables businesses to remain competitive and responsive to changing market conditions. Continuous learning and experimentation foster innovation and improvement in marketing strategies. Engaging with industry communities, attending webinars and conferences, and following thought leaders can provide valuable insights and inspiration.

In conclusion, effective marketing tactics involve a comprehensive approach that combines digital and traditional channels to reach and engage your target market. Understanding your audience, crafting compelling messages, and leveraging various platforms are essential for driving customer acquisition and building brand loyalty. By utilizing strategies such as SEO, social media marketing, email marketing, PPC advertising, influencer marketing, content marketing, and traditional marketing, businesses can create a cohesive and impactful marketing plan. Continuous monitoring, data-driven decision-making, and adaptability ensure that marketing efforts remain relevant and effective in achieving business goals. A well-executed marketing strategy not only enhances visibility and engagement but also fosters long-term customer relationships and brand success.

ppp

"Customer service excellence builds loyalty and retention. Every interaction is an opportunity to impress. Treat customers with respect and care to create lasting relationships."

TWELVE

SALES TECHNIQUES: CONVERTING LEADS INTO CUSTOMERS

Effective sales techniques are essential for converting leads into customers, driving revenue, and ensuring business growth. The sales process involves understanding customer needs, building relationships, presenting solutions, overcoming objections, and closing deals. Mastering these techniques requires a deep understanding of human behavior, strategic planning, and continuous refinement based on feedback and results.

The foundation of successful sales is understanding the customer. This begins with identifying the target audience and understanding their needs, pain points, and motivations. Conducting thorough market research, creating detailed customer personas, and analyzing customer data provide insights into what drives potential buyers. Listening actively during sales interactions is crucial for gaining a deeper understanding of individual customers' specific needs and concerns. By asking open-ended questions and encouraging customers to share their experiences, sales professionals can gather valuable information that guides their approach and helps tailor their pitch.

Building strong relationships with potential customers is a key component of the sales process. Establishing trust and rapport creates a positive environment where customers feel comfortable sharing their needs and concerns. Authenticity, empathy, and transparency are essential for building trust. Sales professionals should focus on genuinely understanding and addressing the customer's needs rather than just pushing a product. Demonstrating empathy involves acknowledging the customer's challenges and showing a sincere interest in helping them find the best solution. Transparency in communication, including being honest about product capabilities and limitations, fosters credibility and trust.

Presenting solutions effectively involves clearly articulating how your product or service addresses the customer's needs and provides value. This requires a deep understanding of the product's features, benefits, and differentiators. Tailoring the presentation to the specific needs and pain points of the customer enhances relevance and impact. Using storytelling to illustrate how the product has helped other customers in similar situations makes the benefits more tangible and relatable. Visual aids, such as demos, videos, and case studies, can enhance the presentation and provide concrete evidence of the product's value.

Handling objections is a critical skill in the sales process. Customers often have concerns or reservations that need to be addressed before they feel confident in making a purchase decision. Effective objection handling involves listening to the customer's concerns, acknowledging their validity, and providing thoughtful responses that alleviate their doubts. It is important to remain calm and composed, view objections as opportunities to provide additional information and reinforce the value of the product. Common objections may relate to price, product fit, or timing. Preparing for these objections in advance and having clear, concise responses ready can help navigate these conversations smoothly.

Negotiation is often a necessary step in closing deals, particularly in B2B sales or high-value transactions. Successful negotiation requires a balance between advocating for your interests and understanding the customer's perspective. Preparation is key, including researching the customer's needs, budget constraints, and decision-making process. Establishing clear objectives and acceptable terms before entering negotiations provides a framework for discussions. Effective negotiators focus on creating win-win outcomes, where both parties feel satisfied with the agreement. Active listening, flexibility, and the ability to articulate the value of concessions are essential skills in negotiation.

Closing the deal is the culmination of the sales process. It involves guiding the customer to make a final purchasing decision and completing the transaction. Various closing techniques can be employed, depending on the situation and the customer's behavior. The assumptive close involves presuming the customer is ready to buy and proceeding with the next steps, such as completing an order form or discussing delivery details. The summary close involves summarizing the key benefits and confirming agreement on each point before asking for the sale. The urgency close leverages time-sensitive offers or incentives to encourage immediate action. Regardless of the technique, confidence and clarity are crucial in the closing phase.

Follow-up is an integral part of the sales process, particularly for complex or high-value sales. Regular follow-up ensures that the customer remains engaged and informed throughout the decision-making process. It also provides opportunities to address any lingering concerns or questions. Personalized follow-up emails, phone calls, or meetings demonstrate a commitment to the customer's success and build stronger relationships. Following up after the sale is equally important for ensuring customer satisfaction, gathering feedback, and identifying opportunities for upselling or cross-selling.

Sales techniques must evolve continuously based on feedback and performance analysis. Regularly reviewing sales metrics, such as conversion rates, average deal size, and sales cycle length, provides insights into the effectiveness of different techniques. Customer feedback, both positive and negative, offers valuable information for refining the sales approach. Sales training and development programs can enhance skills and keep the team updated on best practices and new methodologies. Investing in sales enablement tools, such as customer relationship management (CRM) systems, can streamline the sales process, improve organization, and provide data-driven insights.

The integration of technology in sales has transformed the way sales teams operate and interact with customers. CRM systems, such as Salesforce, HubSpot, or Zoho, provide a centralized platform for managing customer relationships, tracking sales activities, and analyzing performance. These systems enable sales professionals to access customer data, track interactions, and manage follow-up tasks efficiently. Sales automation tools, such as email automation and lead scoring, help prioritize and streamline repetitive tasks, allowing sales teams to focus on high-value activities. Data analytics and AI-powered insights provide actionable recommendations for improving sales strategies and predicting customer behavior.

Social selling leverages social media platforms to connect with potential customers, build relationships, and share valuable content. Platforms like LinkedIn, Twitter, and Facebook offer opportunities to engage with prospects, join industry conversations, and showcase expertise. Social selling involves more than just promoting products; it focuses on providing value through informative content, participating in discussions, and building a personal brand. Sales professionals can use social media to research prospects, understand their needs, and engage with them in meaningful ways. By sharing relevant articles, commenting on industry trends, and providing insights, they can establish themselves as trusted advisors and create opportunities for deeper engagement.

Understanding the buyer's journey is essential for aligning sales techniques with the customer's decision-making process. The buyer's journey typically consists of three stages: awareness, consideration, and decision. During the awareness stage, customers identify a problem or need and begin searching for information. Sales efforts at this stage should focus on providing educational content, raising awareness, and building credibility. In the consideration stage, customers evaluate different solutions and compare options. Sales professionals should provide detailed information, case studies, and demonstrations to help customers make informed comparisons. In the decision stage, customers are ready to choose a solution and make a purchase. At this point, sales efforts should focus on reinforcing the benefits, addressing any final objections, and facilitating a smooth purchasing process.

Personalization is a powerful technique for enhancing the effectiveness of sales efforts. By tailoring interactions and communications to the specific needs and preferences of each customer, sales professionals can create more relevant and engaging experiences. Personalization can be achieved through various means, such as using the customer's name, referencing previous interactions, and providing customized recommendations. Leveraging customer data and insights from CRM systems allows for more precise personalization. Personalized emails, product recommendations, and tailored proposals demonstrate a deep understanding of the customer's needs and build stronger connections.

Building a strong sales culture within the organization is essential for driving consistent performance and achieving sales goals. A positive sales culture fosters collaboration, continuous learning, and a focus on customer success. Encouraging open communication, sharing best practices, and recognizing achievements create a supportive and motivating environment. Providing ongoing training and development opportunities helps sales professionals enhance their skills and stay updated on industry trends and techniques. Setting clear goals, providing regular feedback, and celebrating successes contribute to a high-performance sales culture.

Collaboration between sales and marketing teams is crucial for ensuring alignment and maximizing the effectiveness of sales efforts. Marketing teams generate leads, create content, and build brand awareness, while sales teams convert leads into customers. Close collaboration ensures that both teams are working towards common goals and sharing insights to improve performance. Regular meetings, shared goals, and integrated tools facilitate communication and coordination. Marketing can provide valuable resources, such as lead nurturing content and campaign analytics, to support the sales process. Sales can offer feedback on lead quality and customer insights to refine marketing strategies.

Ethical sales practices are fundamental for building long-term customer relationships and maintaining a positive reputation. Sales professionals should prioritize honesty, transparency, and integrity in all interactions. Misleading claims, high-pressure tactics, and manipulative techniques can damage trust and lead to negative outcomes. Ethical sales practices involve providing accurate information, respecting customer decisions, and focusing on delivering genuine value. Building a reputation for ethical behavior enhances credibility, fosters customer loyalty, and contributes to sustainable business growth.

In conclusion, effective sales techniques involve a comprehensive approach that includes understanding customer needs, building relationships, presenting solutions, handling objections, negotiating, and closing deals. Personalization, follow-up, and continuous improvement are essential for maintaining high performance and driving revenue. The integration of technology, social selling, and alignment with the buyer's journey enhances the effectiveness of sales efforts. Building a strong sales culture, fostering collaboration with marketing, and adhering to ethical practices contribute to long-term success. By mastering these techniques and continuously refining their approach, sales professionals can convert leads into loyal customers and achieve business growth.

▷▷▷

"Operational efficiency is the backbone of a successful business. Streamline processes to enhance productivity. Efficiency saves resources and drives growth."

THIRTEEN

CUSTOMER SERVICE EXCELLENCE: BUILDING LOYALTY AND RETENTION

Customer service excellence is a cornerstone of business success, playing a critical role in building loyalty and retention. In a competitive market, where products and services can often be replicated, exceptional customer service sets a business apart. It transforms customers into loyal advocates who not only return for repeat business but also refer others, thereby driving growth through positive word-of-mouth. Achieving excellence in customer service requires a comprehensive approach that encompasses understanding customer needs, training staff, creating seamless experiences, and continuously improving based on feedback and metrics.

Understanding customer needs is the first step in delivering exceptional service. This involves gathering and analyzing data on customer preferences, behaviors, and feedback. Businesses can use surveys, focus groups, customer interviews, and analytics tools to gain insights into what customers value and what their pain points are. By segmenting customers based on their needs and preferences, businesses can tailor their service approach to different groups. For example, some customers may prioritize speed and efficiency, while others may value personalized interactions and detailed information. Understanding these nuances allows businesses to deliver a more targeted and satisfying experience.

Training staff is crucial for ensuring that every customer interaction reflects the business's commitment to excellence. Customer service representatives are the frontline ambassadors of a brand, and their skills and attitudes significantly impact customer perceptions. Comprehensive training programs should cover product knowledge, communication skills, problem-solving techniques, and emotional intelligence. Employees should be trained to listen actively, empathize with customers, and respond effectively to their needs. Role-playing exercises, simulations, and real-time feedback can help staff practice and refine their skills. Continuous training and development ensure that employees stay updated on best practices and new technologies.

Creating seamless and positive customer experiences involves designing processes and systems that make it easy for customers to interact with the business. This includes everything from website navigation and online purchasing to in-store interactions and after-sales support. A user-friendly website with clear information, easy navigation, and responsive design ensures that customers can find what they need quickly and easily. Offering multiple communication channels, such as phone, email, live chat, and social media, provides customers with convenient options for reaching out. Ensuring consistency and integration across these channels, known as omnichannel support, helps create a cohesive and smooth experience.

Proactive customer service is a powerful way to anticipate and address customer needs before they become issues. This involves reaching out to customers with helpful information, reminders, and updates. For example, sending notifications about order status, delivery times, or product recalls demonstrates attentiveness and care. Personalized recommendations based on past purchases can enhance the customer experience and drive additional sales. By proactively addressing potential problems, such as service interruptions or product shortages, businesses can minimize frustration and build trust.

Handling customer complaints effectively is essential for maintaining trust and loyalty. Complaints should be viewed as opportunities to improve and strengthen customer relationships. When customers voice their concerns, they want to be heard, understood, and reassured that their issues will be resolved. Responding quickly and empathetically is crucial. Acknowledging the problem, apologizing for any inconvenience, and providing a clear resolution plan helps turn a negative experience into a positive one. Empowering customer service representatives to make decisions and resolve issues on the spot can speed up the resolution process and enhance customer satisfaction. Follow-up communication to ensure that the problem has been resolved satisfactorily demonstrates commitment to customer care.

Building a customer-centric culture within the organization is fundamental to achieving service excellence. This involves aligning the entire business around the goal of delivering exceptional customer experiences. Leadership plays a critical role in setting the tone and fostering a culture that values and prioritizes customers. Recognizing and rewarding employees who go above and beyond in serving customers reinforces the importance of customer service. Encouraging cross-departmental collaboration ensures that customer service is integrated into all aspects of the business, from product development to marketing to logistics.

Leveraging technology can enhance customer service by improving efficiency and personalization. Customer relationship management (CRM) systems, such as Salesforce or HubSpot, provide a centralized platform for managing customer interactions and data. These systems enable businesses to track customer history, preferences, and feedback, allowing for more personalized and informed service. Automation tools, such as chatbots and automated email responses, can handle routine inquiries and free up human agents to focus on more complex issues. AI-powered analytics can provide insights into customer behavior and predict future needs, helping businesses tailor their service approach.

Measuring and analyzing customer service performance is essential for continuous improvement. Key performance indicators (KPIs) such as customer satisfaction (CSAT) scores, Net Promoter Score (NPS), and first response time provide valuable insights into how well the business is meeting customer needs. Regularly collecting and reviewing feedback from surveys, reviews, and social media helps identify strengths and areas for improvement. Advanced analytics can uncover patterns and trends in customer interactions, guiding strategic decisions and process enhancements. Benchmarking performance against industry standards and competitors provides context and helps set realistic goals.

Customer loyalty programs are effective tools for building long-term relationships and rewarding repeat customers. These programs can include points-based systems, tiered rewards, exclusive discounts, and personalized offers. By providing tangible benefits, loyalty programs incentivize customers to return and make additional purchases. Personalization is key to the success of loyalty programs; tailoring rewards and communications to individual preferences enhances the perceived value and relevance. Engaging customers through regular updates, special events, and community-building activities strengthens their connection to the brand.

Creating memorable customer experiences is about exceeding expectations and delivering moments of delight. Small gestures, such as personalized thank-you notes, surprise discounts, or complimentary services, can leave a lasting impression. Recognizing and celebrating customer milestones, such as anniversaries or birthdays, adds a personal touch. Going the extra mile to solve a problem or fulfill a special request demonstrates genuine care and commitment. These positive experiences not only foster loyalty but also encourage customers to share their stories with others, generating valuable word-of-mouth promotion.

Transparency and honesty are fundamental to building trust with customers. Being open about product capabilities, pricing, policies, and any potential issues fosters credibility. When problems arise, such as delays or defects, proactively communicating with customers and providing clear updates helps manage expectations and maintain trust. Transparency in data privacy and security practices is also crucial in today's digital age. Customers want to know how their information is being used and protected, and businesses that prioritize data security earn their trust and confidence.

Engaging with customers through social media provides opportunities for real-time interaction and relationship building. Social media platforms allow businesses to share updates, respond to inquiries, and participate in conversations with customers. Monitoring social media for mentions and feedback enables timely responses and demonstrates attentiveness. Creating and sharing engaging content, such as tutorials, behind-the-scenes looks, and customer stories, fosters community and brand loyalty. Social media also serves as a platform for addressing customer service issues publicly, showcasing the business's commitment to resolving problems and valuing customer input.

Encouraging and acting on customer feedback is essential for continuous improvement. Customers provide valuable insights into their experiences, preferences, and expectations. Actively seeking feedback through surveys, reviews, and direct interactions helps businesses understand what they are doing well and where they can improve. It is important to act on this feedback, making tangible changes and communicating these improvements to customers. This demonstrates that the business values customer input and is committed to enhancing their experience.

Building long-term customer relationships involves consistently delivering value and maintaining engagement. Regular communication through newsletters, personalized emails, and updates keeps customers informed and connected. Offering exclusive content, early access to new products, and special events strengthens the relationship and reinforces loyalty. Providing exceptional after-sales support, such as easy returns, warranty services, and ongoing assistance, ensures that customers feel supported throughout their journey with the brand.

Fostering a sense of community among customers enhances loyalty and retention. Creating opportunities for customers to connect with each other and the brand builds a supportive and engaged community. Online forums, social media groups, and in-person events provide platforms for interaction and sharing. Encouraging user-generated content, such as reviews, photos, and stories, highlights customer experiences and builds authenticity. Recognizing and celebrating customer contributions fosters a sense of belonging and strengthens the emotional connection to the brand.

In summary, customer service excellence is a multifaceted approach that involves understanding customer needs, training staff, creating seamless experiences, and continuously improving based on feedback and metrics. Building strong relationships, handling complaints effectively, and fostering a customer-centric culture are essential components. Leveraging technology, personalizing interactions, and measuring performance enhance service delivery. Transparency, engaging through social media, and encouraging feedback build trust and drive continuous improvement. Loyalty programs, memorable experiences, and fostering community strengthen long-term relationships. By prioritizing customer service excellence, businesses can build loyalty, drive retention, and achieve sustainable growth.

ppp

"Building a strong team is crucial for achieving your goals. Hire for skill and cultural fit. A motivated team is your greatest asset."

FOURTEEN

Operational Efficiency: Streamlining Your Processes

Operational efficiency is crucial for the sustainability and growth of any business. It involves optimizing various processes to reduce waste, improve productivity, and enhance overall performance. Streamlining operations can lead to cost savings, better resource utilization, higher customer satisfaction, and a stronger competitive position. Achieving operational efficiency requires a strategic approach that encompasses process analysis, technology integration, employee engagement, and continuous improvement.

The first step in improving operational efficiency is to analyze existing processes. This involves mapping out workflows, identifying bottlenecks, and understanding how different tasks are interconnected. Process mapping provides a visual representation of how work flows through the organization, highlighting areas where delays, redundancies, or inefficiencies occur. Tools such as flowcharts, process diagrams, and value stream mapping can aid in this analysis. Engaging employees who are directly involved in these processes is essential, as they can offer valuable insights into day-to-day operations and potential areas for improvement.

Once processes are mapped and analyzed, the next step is to identify opportunities for improvement. This may involve eliminating non-value-added activities, automating repetitive tasks, or reconfiguring workflows to enhance productivity. Lean principles, which focus on maximizing value while minimizing waste, can guide this effort. Lean methodologies emphasize continuous improvement, employee involvement, and a customer-centric approach. Techniques such as the 5S framework (Sort, Set in order, Shine, Standardize, Sustain) and Kaizen (continuous improvement) can help streamline processes and foster a culture of efficiency.

Technology integration plays a significant role in enhancing operational efficiency. Automation tools, software solutions, and advanced technologies can streamline processes, reduce manual errors, and free up employees to focus on higher-value tasks. Enterprise Resource Planning (ERP) systems, for example, integrate various business functions such as finance, human resources, supply chain, and manufacturing into a single platform. This integration facilitates real-time data sharing, improves decision-making, and enhances overall coordination. Customer Relationship Management (CRM) systems streamline sales, marketing, and customer service processes, providing a unified view of customer interactions and enabling more personalized and efficient service.

The adoption of automation technologies can significantly reduce the time and effort required for routine tasks. Robotic Process Automation (RPA) uses software robots to perform repetitive tasks such as data entry, invoice processing, and order fulfillment. RPA can operate around the clock, ensuring consistency and accuracy while freeing up human employees for more strategic activities.

Artificial Intelligence (AI) and machine learning can further enhance efficiency by analyzing large volumes of data, identifying patterns, and making predictions. AI-powered chatbots, for example, can handle customer inquiries, provide instant responses, and escalate complex issues to human agents when necessary.

Employee engagement is a critical factor in achieving operational efficiency. Employees who are motivated, empowered, and aligned with the organization's goals are more likely to contribute to process improvements and maintain high levels of productivity. Creating a culture of continuous improvement involves encouraging employees to identify inefficiencies, suggest solutions, and participate in decision-making. Providing training and development opportunities ensures that employees have the skills and knowledge needed to adapt to new technologies and processes. Recognizing and rewarding contributions to efficiency improvements reinforces positive behavior and fosters a sense of ownership.

Effective communication and collaboration are essential for streamlining operations. Clear communication ensures that employees understand their roles, responsibilities, and how their work contributes to overall efficiency. Collaboration tools such as project management software, instant messaging platforms, and video conferencing facilitate teamwork and coordination, especially in remote or distributed work environments. Regular meetings, progress updates, and feedback sessions help keep everyone aligned and informed.

Supply chain management is another critical area where operational efficiency can be improved. A well-managed supply chain ensures that materials and products are available when needed, reducing delays and inventory costs. Implementing Just-In-Time (JIT) inventory management minimizes excess inventory and reduces storage costs. Advanced supply chain analytics provide insights into demand patterns, supplier performance, and logistics, enabling more accurate forecasting and planning. Building strong relationships with suppliers and partners enhances collaboration and ensures a more resilient and responsive supply chain.

Quality management is integral to operational efficiency, as defects, rework, and waste can significantly impact productivity and costs. Implementing a robust quality management system (QMS) ensures that processes are designed to meet quality standards and that any deviations are promptly identified and addressed. Techniques such as Six Sigma, which focuses on reducing variability and improving process capability, can enhance quality and efficiency. Total Quality Management (TQM) involves a holistic approach to quality, emphasizing continuous improvement, customer focus, and employee involvement.

Data-driven decision-making is essential for optimizing operations. Collecting and analyzing data from various processes provides insights into performance, identifies trends, and highlights areas for improvement. Key performance indicators (KPIs) such as cycle time, throughput, defect rates, and customer satisfaction measure efficiency and effectiveness. Using dashboards and data visualization tools, managers can monitor KPIs in real-time and make informed decisions. Predictive analytics and business intelligence tools leverage historical data to forecast future trends and optimize resource allocation.

Energy efficiency is an often-overlooked aspect of operational efficiency. Reducing energy consumption not only lowers costs but also contributes to environmental sustainability. Implementing energy-efficient technologies, optimizing equipment usage, and adopting renewable energy sources can enhance operational efficiency. Regular energy audits identify opportunities for improvement, and energy management systems monitor and control energy usage in real-time.

Standardization is a key strategy for improving operational efficiency. Standardizing processes ensures consistency, reduces variability, and simplifies training. Developing standard operating procedures (SOPs) provides clear guidelines for performing tasks, ensuring that everyone follows best practices. Documenting and regularly reviewing SOPs ensures that they remain relevant and effective. Standardization also facilitates scalability, as standardized processes can be more easily replicated and expanded.

Customer feedback is a valuable source of insights for improving operational efficiency. Listening to customers' experiences, suggestions, and complaints helps identify areas where processes can be enhanced to better meet their needs. Implementing a systematic approach to collecting and analyzing customer feedback, such as surveys, focus groups, and online reviews, ensures that the voice of the customer is integrated into process improvement efforts. Addressing customer feedback promptly and effectively enhances satisfaction and loyalty.

Change management is crucial for the successful implementation of efficiency initiatives. Changes to processes, technologies, or organizational structures can face resistance from employees. Effective change management involves clear communication, employee involvement, and support throughout the transition. Explaining the reasons for change, the benefits it brings, and how it aligns with organizational goals helps build buy-in. Providing training and resources to support employees during the transition ensures a smoother implementation.

Outsourcing non-core activities can also enhance operational efficiency by allowing the organization to focus on its core competencies. Activities such as payroll processing, IT support, and customer service can be outsourced to specialized providers who can perform them more efficiently. Outsourcing can reduce costs, improve service quality, and provide access to expertise and advanced technologies. However, it is essential to carefully select outsourcing partners and establish clear contracts and performance metrics to ensure alignment with organizational goals.

Continuous improvement is a fundamental principle of operational efficiency. The Plan-Do-Check-Act (PDCA) cycle, also known as the Deming Cycle, provides a structured approach to continuous improvement. It involves planning changes based on data and analysis, implementing changes on a small scale, checking the results, and acting based on the findings. Iterative cycles of improvement ensure that processes are continuously optimized and that efficiency gains are sustained over time.

Employee well-being is an important consideration in achieving operational efficiency. A healthy and motivated workforce is more productive and engaged. Providing a safe and comfortable working environment, promoting work-life balance, and offering wellness programs contribute to employee well-being. Regularly assessing and addressing factors that impact employee satisfaction and morale ensures a positive and productive workplace.

Benchmarking against industry standards and best practices provides insights into how well the organization is performing relative to competitors. Identifying and adopting best practices from leading organizations helps drive improvements and innovation. Benchmarking also provides a basis for setting realistic and achievable goals for operational efficiency.

In conclusion, operational efficiency is essential for business success and involves optimizing processes, leveraging technology, engaging employees, and fostering a culture of continuous improvement. Analyzing and mapping processes, integrating automation and advanced technologies, and standardizing procedures enhance productivity and reduce waste. Effective communication, collaboration, and change management ensure smooth implementation of efficiency initiatives. Engaging employees, listening to customer feedback, and prioritizing quality management drive sustainable improvements. By focusing on operational efficiency, businesses can achieve cost savings, improve customer satisfaction, and maintain a competitive edge in the market. Continuous monitoring, data-driven decision-making, and a commitment to excellence ensure that efficiency gains are sustained and that the organization remains agile and responsive to changing conditions.

❧❧❧

"Financial management is the cornerstone of business sustainability. Plan, budget, and monitor performance. Sound financial practices ensure long-term success."

FIFTEEN

TEAM BUILDING: HIRING AND MANAGING YOUR STAFF

Team building is fundamental to the success of any organization, as the people who make up your team are the driving force behind your business's performance, innovation, and growth. Effective team building involves hiring the right individuals, fostering a collaborative and inclusive environment, and implementing management practices that motivate and engage employees. This process requires careful planning, strategic decision-making, and a commitment to creating a culture that supports and nurtures talent.

The first step in building a successful team is hiring the right people. This begins with a clear understanding of the roles and responsibilities needed to achieve your business objectives. Creating detailed job descriptions that outline the required skills, qualifications, and experience helps attract suitable candidates. It is essential to define not only the technical competencies needed but also the soft skills and cultural fit that align with your organization's values and work environment.

The recruitment process should be thorough and structured to ensure you identify the best candidates. This involves multiple stages, including resume screening, phone interviews, and in-person or virtual interviews. During interviews, ask open-ended questions that allow candidates to demonstrate their skills, experience, and problem-solving abilities. Behavioral interview questions, which focus on past experiences and actions, can provide insights into how candidates might perform in similar situations within your organization. Additionally, assessing cultural fit is crucial, as employees who align with your organization's values and culture are more likely to thrive and contribute positively.

Leveraging technology can enhance the recruitment process. Applicant tracking systems (ATS) streamline the management of job applications and help identify the most promising candidates. Video interview platforms enable remote interviews, expanding your talent pool beyond geographical limitations. Social media and professional networks like LinkedIn are valuable tools for sourcing candidates and building a strong employer brand. Employee referrals can also be an effective recruitment strategy, as current employees can recommend candidates who they believe will be a good fit for the organization.

Onboarding is a critical phase in the hiring process that sets the tone for a new employee's experience and integration into the team. A structured onboarding program helps new hires understand their roles, the organization's culture, and the expectations for their performance. This includes orientation sessions, training programs, and meetings with key team members. Providing a mentor or buddy can help new employees navigate the initial period and feel supported. Effective onboarding accelerates the time to productivity and enhances employee retention by making new hires feel valued and welcomed.

Once you have built a team, fostering a collaborative and inclusive environment is essential for maximizing their potential. Collaboration involves creating opportunities for team members to work together, share ideas, and leverage each other's strengths. Encouraging open communication and transparency builds trust and fosters a culture of mutual respect. Regular team meetings, brainstorming sessions, and collaborative projects facilitate interaction and knowledge sharing.

Inclusion is about ensuring that all team members feel valued, respected, and able to contribute to their fullest potential. This involves embracing diversity in all its forms, including differences in background, perspective, and experience. Creating an inclusive environment requires proactive efforts to eliminate biases, provide equal opportunities, and support the unique needs of each team member. Providing diversity and inclusion training, establishing employee resource groups, and promoting inclusive policies and practices are key steps in building an inclusive workplace.

Effective management is crucial for maintaining a motivated and high-performing team. This involves setting clear goals and expectations, providing regular feedback, and recognizing and rewarding achievements. Clear and achievable goals give employees a sense of direction and purpose. These goals should be aligned with the organization's objectives and communicated clearly to ensure everyone understands their role in achieving them. Setting SMART (Specific, Measurable, Achievable, Relevant, Time-bound) goals helps ensure they are realistic and attainable.

Providing regular feedback is essential for continuous improvement and development. Constructive feedback helps employees understand their strengths and areas for growth, while positive feedback and recognition reinforce desired behaviors and achievements. Conducting regular performance reviews and one-on-one meetings provides structured opportunities for feedback and discussion. These meetings should be a two-way dialogue, where employees feel comfortable sharing their thoughts, concerns, and aspirations.

Recognizing and rewarding achievements is a powerful motivator. This can take various forms, from verbal praise and written acknowledgments to financial incentives and career advancement opportunities. Recognizing individual and team accomplishments fosters a sense of achievement and encourages continued excellence. It is important to ensure that recognition is timely, specific, and meaningful to the recipient.

Professional development is another critical aspect of effective management. Providing opportunities for learning and growth not only enhances employees' skills and capabilities but also demonstrates a commitment to their long-term success. This can include on-the-job training, workshops, courses, and access to industry conferences. Supporting career development through mentorship, coaching, and clear career paths helps employees envision their future within the organization and stay motivated.

Creating a positive work environment is essential for employee satisfaction and retention. This involves ensuring that the workplace is physically comfortable, safe, and conducive to productivity. Additionally, fostering a positive organizational culture that promotes work-life balance, mental well-being, and a sense of community enhances overall job satisfaction. Offering flexible work arrangements, wellness programs, and team-building activities contributes to a supportive and engaging work environment.

Conflict resolution is an important skill for managers, as conflicts are inevitable in any workplace. Addressing conflicts promptly and effectively prevents them from escalating and negatively impacting team dynamics. This involves understanding the root cause of the conflict, facilitating open and respectful communication, and working collaboratively to find a resolution. Encouraging a culture of respect and empathy helps prevent conflicts and promotes a harmonious work environment.

Adaptability and resilience are essential qualities for both managers and team members in today's fast-paced and ever-changing business landscape. Encouraging a growth mindset, where challenges are viewed as opportunities for learning and improvement, fosters resilience. Supporting employees through changes, whether they involve new technologies, processes, or organizational structures, helps build adaptability. Providing training, resources, and clear communication during times of change ensures that employees feel prepared and supported.

Building a cohesive and high-performing team also involves fostering a sense of purpose and alignment with the organization's mission and values. When employees understand and connect with the organization's purpose, they are more likely to be engaged and motivated. Communicating the organization's vision, mission, and values clearly and consistently helps create a shared sense of purpose. Involving employees in decision-making processes and seeking their input on organizational initiatives fosters a sense of ownership and commitment.

Regularly assessing and refining team-building practices ensures that they remain effective and aligned with the organization's goals. This involves soliciting feedback from employees, monitoring key performance indicators (KPIs), and staying informed about best practices and industry trends. Adapting and evolving team-building strategies based on feedback and data helps maintain a dynamic and responsive approach.

In summary, team building is a multifaceted process that involves hiring the right people, fostering a collaborative and inclusive environment, and implementing effective management practices. By understanding and addressing the needs of your team, providing opportunities for growth and development, and creating a positive work environment, you can build a motivated and high-performing team. Clear communication, regular feedback, recognition, and conflict resolution are essential components of effective management. Embracing diversity, promoting inclusion, and fostering a sense of purpose enhance team cohesion and engagement. Continuous assessment and refinement of team-building practices ensure that they remain relevant and effective in achieving organizational success. A strong team is the foundation of a successful organization, driving innovation, performance, and growth.

ppp

*"Scaling up requires strategic planning and
resource management. Maintain quality and values
as you grow. Expansion should be sustainable and
well-managed."*

SIXTEEN

FINANCIAL MANAGEMENT: KEEPING YOUR BUSINESS PROFITABLE

Financial management is crucial for the sustainability and growth of any business. It involves planning, organizing, controlling, and monitoring financial resources to achieve business objectives. Effective financial management ensures that a business remains profitable, can meet its obligations, and has the resources necessary for growth and innovation. It encompasses budgeting, forecasting, cash flow management, investment decisions, and financial analysis.

The foundation of financial management is a robust budgeting process. A budget is a financial plan that outlines expected revenues, expenses, and capital expenditures over a specific period. It serves as a roadmap for the business, guiding decision-making and ensuring that resources are allocated effectively. Creating a budget involves analyzing historical financial data, understanding market conditions, and setting realistic goals. It requires input from various departments to ensure that all aspects of the business are considered. Regularly reviewing and updating the budget helps keep the business on track and allows for adjustments in response to changes in the market or business environment.

Forecasting is closely related to budgeting and involves predicting future financial performance based on historical data and market trends. Accurate forecasting helps businesses anticipate challenges, identify opportunities, and make informed decisions. It includes projections for sales, expenses, cash flow, and capital needs. Different forecasting techniques, such as trend analysis, regression analysis, and scenario planning, can be used to develop reliable forecasts. Regularly comparing actual performance against forecasts allows businesses to identify variances and take corrective actions.

Cash flow management is a critical aspect of financial management, as it ensures that a business has sufficient liquidity to meet its short-term obligations. Positive cash flow indicates that a business can pay its bills, invest in growth opportunities, and cushion against unexpected expenses. Effective cash flow management involves monitoring cash inflows and outflows, optimizing working capital, and maintaining a buffer of liquid assets. Strategies such as offering early payment discounts to customers, negotiating favorable payment terms with suppliers, and regularly reviewing inventory levels can improve cash flow. Using cash flow forecasts helps businesses plan for periods of high and low liquidity and take proactive measures to manage cash effectively.

Investment decisions are another key component of financial management. These decisions involve allocating capital to projects, assets, or initiatives that are expected to generate returns and contribute to the business's growth. Evaluating investment opportunities requires a thorough analysis of potential risks and returns. Tools such as net present value (NPV), internal rate of return (IRR), and payback period are commonly used to assess the profitability and feasibility of investments. Diversifying investments across different projects or asset classes can help mitigate risks and enhance overall returns.

Financial analysis is essential for understanding the financial health and performance of a business. It involves analyzing financial statements, such as the income statement, balance sheet, and cash flow statement, to gain insights into profitability, liquidity, solvency, and efficiency. Key financial ratios, such as gross profit margin, net profit margin, current ratio, debt-to-equity ratio, and return on equity, provide valuable benchmarks for assessing performance. Regular financial analysis helps identify trends, strengths, and weaknesses, guiding strategic decisions and operational improvements.

Cost management is a critical aspect of maintaining profitability. It involves identifying, analyzing, and controlling costs to ensure that they align with the business's financial goals. This includes both fixed costs, such as rent and salaries, and variable costs, such as raw materials and production expenses. Implementing cost control measures, such as optimizing procurement processes, reducing waste, and improving operational efficiency, can significantly impact the bottom line. Activity-based costing (ABC) is a method that allocates costs to specific activities, providing a more accurate picture of where resources are being consumed and highlighting areas for cost reduction.

Pricing strategy is another important factor in financial management. Setting the right prices for products or services involves understanding market demand, competitor pricing, and the perceived value to customers. A well-designed pricing strategy ensures that prices cover costs and generate a reasonable profit margin while remaining competitive. Different pricing strategies, such as cost-plus pricing, value-based pricing, and dynamic pricing, can be employed based on the nature of the business and market conditions. Regularly reviewing and adjusting prices in response to changes in costs, demand, and competition helps maintain profitability.

Managing debt is a crucial aspect of financial management. While debt can provide necessary capital for growth and expansion, excessive debt can strain cash flow and increase financial risk. Effective debt management involves evaluating the cost of debt, maintaining a balanced debt-to-equity ratio, and ensuring that debt servicing obligations can be met without compromising operational stability. Refinancing high-interest debt, negotiating favorable terms with lenders, and using debt strategically to finance high-return investments are important considerations for managing debt effectively.

Tax planning is an essential component of financial management, as it helps businesses minimize tax liabilities and ensure compliance with tax regulations. Effective tax planning involves understanding applicable tax laws, taking advantage of tax credits and deductions, and strategically timing income and expenses to optimize tax outcomes. Working with tax professionals can provide valuable insights and help navigate complex tax issues. Regularly reviewing and updating tax strategies in response to changes in tax laws and business circumstances ensures ongoing compliance and efficiency.

Maintaining adequate insurance coverage is important for protecting the business against potential financial losses due to unforeseen events. Insurance policies such as property insurance, liability insurance, and business interruption insurance provide a safety net and help mitigate risks. Regularly reviewing insurance coverage and making adjustments based on changes in business operations, asset values, and risk exposure ensures that the business remains adequately protected.

Building and maintaining strong relationships with financial institutions, investors, and stakeholders is essential for effective financial management. These relationships provide access to capital, financial advice, and support during challenging times. Transparent communication, regular financial reporting, and demonstrating sound financial practices help build trust and credibility with stakeholders. Engaging with financial advisors and consultants can provide additional expertise and perspectives on financial strategies and decisions.

Financial planning for growth and expansion involves assessing the financial implications of scaling operations, entering new markets, or launching new products. This includes evaluating the required capital investment, projected revenues and expenses, and potential risks. Developing a detailed financial plan that outlines the funding sources, cash flow projections, and expected returns helps guide strategic growth initiatives. Securing funding for growth may involve a combination of internal funds, external financing, and reinvested profits. Maintaining financial discipline and monitoring performance against the growth plan ensures that expansion efforts are sustainable and aligned with the business's long-term goals.

Risk management is an integral part of financial management, as it involves identifying, assessing, and mitigating financial risks that could impact the business's stability and profitability. This includes market risks, credit risks, operational risks, and liquidity risks. Implementing risk management strategies, such as diversifying revenue streams, maintaining sufficient liquidity, and hedging against market fluctuations, helps protect the business from adverse financial impacts. Regular risk assessments and scenario planning provide insights into potential vulnerabilities and guide the development of contingency plans.

Corporate governance and ethical financial practices are fundamental to maintaining trust and integrity in financial management. Establishing clear governance structures, internal controls, and compliance procedures ensures that financial practices are transparent, accountable, and aligned with legal and regulatory requirements. Promoting a culture of ethical behavior and integrity in financial decision-making fosters a positive reputation and builds stakeholder confidence. Regular audits and reviews provide assurance that financial practices are sound and that risks are managed effectively.

Adopting technology and digital tools can enhance financial management by improving efficiency, accuracy, and decision-making. Financial management software, such as accounting systems, budgeting tools, and financial analytics platforms, streamline processes and provide real-time insights into financial performance. Automation of routine tasks, such as invoicing, payroll, and expense tracking, reduces errors and frees up time for strategic financial planning. Leveraging data analytics and artificial intelligence can provide deeper insights into financial trends, forecast future performance, and optimize resource allocation.

Succession planning and financial continuity are important considerations for ensuring the long-term sustainability of the business. This involves identifying and developing future leaders, establishing clear succession plans, and ensuring that financial management practices are institutionalized rather than dependent on specific individuals. Planning for transitions, whether due to retirement, unexpected events, or strategic changes, ensures that the business can continue to operate smoothly and maintain financial stability.

In conclusion, effective financial management is essential for keeping a business profitable and sustainable. It involves a comprehensive approach that includes budgeting, forecasting, cash flow management, investment decisions, financial analysis, cost management, pricing strategy, debt management, tax planning, insurance, stakeholder relationships, growth planning, risk management, corporate governance, and the adoption of technology. By implementing sound financial practices and continuously monitoring and adapting strategies, businesses can achieve financial stability, support growth, and navigate challenges. Financial management is a dynamic and ongoing process that requires vigilance, strategic thinking, and a commitment to excellence.

❦❦❦

"Overcoming challenges requires resilience and adaptability. Learn from setbacks and keep moving forward. Every challenge is an opportunity to grow stronger."

SEVENTEEN

SCALING UP: GROWING YOUR BUSINESS SUSTAINABLY

Scaling up a business is a pivotal phase that involves expanding operations, increasing revenue, and entering new markets while ensuring sustainability and maintaining the core values and quality that initially defined the business. Sustainable growth requires strategic planning, effective resource management, and a keen understanding of the market dynamics and operational challenges. It is a balancing act of seizing opportunities for expansion while safeguarding the business against potential risks.

The foundation of sustainable growth is a clear and comprehensive growth strategy. This strategy outlines the goals, target markets, competitive positioning, and the resources required to achieve expansion. A well-defined growth plan begins with a thorough market analysis to identify opportunities and threats. Understanding customer needs, market trends, and the competitive landscape helps businesses make informed decisions about where and how to expand. Identifying new customer segments, exploring geographic markets, and diversifying product or service offerings can provide avenues for growth.

A key aspect of scaling up is ensuring that the business infrastructure can support increased demand. This involves evaluating and enhancing the operational capacity, including production, supply chain, technology, and human resources. Investing in scalable systems and processes is essential. For example, upgrading technology infrastructure, automating workflows, and implementing robust project management tools can enhance efficiency and reduce bottlenecks. Ensuring that supply chains are flexible and reliable is crucial to meet increased production and distribution demands without compromising quality.

Financial management plays a critical role in sustainable growth. Scaling up often requires significant investment, whether in new facilities, technology, marketing, or talent. Effective financial planning involves securing the necessary capital while maintaining healthy cash flow and managing debt levels. Businesses may explore various funding options, such as reinvesting profits, seeking venture capital, or securing loans. It is essential to create detailed financial projections that account for increased expenses and potential revenue growth. Monitoring key financial metrics, such as profit margins, return on investment, and cash flow, provides insights into the financial health of the business and helps make informed decisions.

Human resources are a vital component of scaling up. As the business grows, so does the need for a skilled and capable workforce. Recruiting and retaining talent becomes increasingly important. Building a strong team that aligns with the company's vision and values is crucial for sustaining growth. This involves not only hiring new employees but also investing in the development of existing staff. Providing training, mentorship, and career advancement opportunities enhances employee engagement and productivity. Creating a positive work environment that fosters collaboration, innovation, and job satisfaction helps attract and retain top talent.

Maintaining the quality and consistency of products or services during growth is essential to protect the brand reputation. Rapid expansion can strain resources and processes, leading to potential quality issues. Implementing rigorous quality control measures and continuously monitoring performance ensures that standards are upheld. Customer feedback is invaluable for identifying areas for improvement and ensuring that the business continues to meet or exceed customer expectations. Building strong relationships with customers and addressing their needs and concerns promptly reinforces loyalty and trust.

Marketing and sales strategies must evolve to support growth. Expanding into new markets requires tailored marketing approaches that resonate with different customer segments. Developing a strong brand presence and leveraging digital marketing channels, such as social media, content marketing, and search engine optimization, can increase visibility and attract new customers. Data-driven marketing strategies, including targeted advertising and personalized campaigns, enhance engagement and conversion rates. A scalable sales strategy involves optimizing the sales process, leveraging technology, and building a capable sales team that can effectively manage increased leads and opportunities.

Innovation and continuous improvement are fundamental to sustaining growth. Businesses must stay ahead of industry trends, embrace new technologies, and continuously refine their products, services, and processes. Encouraging a culture of innovation where employees are empowered to suggest and implement improvements fosters creativity and adaptability. Regularly reviewing and updating business practices ensures that the company remains competitive and responsive to market changes. Investing in research and development can lead to new product offerings and enhancements that drive further growth.

Strategic partnerships and collaborations can accelerate growth and provide access to new markets, technologies, and expertise. Forming alliances with other businesses, suppliers, or industry organizations can enhance capabilities and expand reach. For example, partnering with a company that has a strong distribution network can facilitate market entry and increase sales. Collaborations on research and development projects can lead to innovative solutions and shared resources. It is important to carefully evaluate potential partners and ensure that the collaboration aligns with the business's strategic goals and values.

Risk management is a critical aspect of scaling up. Growth brings new challenges and uncertainties, and it is essential to identify and mitigate potential risks. This includes financial risks, operational risks, market risks, and regulatory risks. Developing a comprehensive risk management plan that outlines potential threats and strategies for mitigation ensures that the business is prepared for various scenarios. Regularly reviewing and updating the risk management plan based on changing conditions helps maintain resilience and stability.

Sustainability is increasingly important in today's business environment. Growing a business sustainably involves considering the environmental and social impacts of expansion. Implementing sustainable practices, such as reducing waste, optimizing energy use, and sourcing materials responsibly, can enhance the business's reputation and appeal to socially conscious consumers. Corporate social responsibility (CSR) initiatives that contribute to the community and support social causes can strengthen brand loyalty and differentiate the business from competitors. Sustainability should be integrated into the business strategy, with clear goals and metrics to track progress.

Customer relationships are at the heart of sustainable growth. Building and maintaining strong relationships with customers involves understanding their needs, providing exceptional service, and delivering consistent value. Customer loyalty programs, personalized experiences, and proactive communication enhance customer satisfaction and retention. Gathering and acting on customer feedback ensures that the business remains attuned to changing preferences and expectations. Loyal customers not only provide repeat business but also become advocates who refer others and contribute to positive word-of-mouth marketing.

Corporate governance and ethical practices are fundamental to sustainable growth. Strong governance structures, transparent decision-making, and adherence to ethical standards build trust with stakeholders, including customers, employees, investors, and regulators. Establishing clear policies and procedures, conducting regular audits, and fostering a culture of integrity ensures compliance with legal and regulatory requirements. Ethical business practices enhance reputation, reduce risks, and contribute to long-term success.

Flexibility and adaptability are crucial for navigating the complexities of growth. Businesses must be prepared to pivot and adjust their strategies based on market conditions, customer feedback, and emerging opportunities. This requires a mindset of continuous learning and improvement. Embracing change and being open to new ideas and approaches enables businesses to remain competitive and resilient. Regularly reviewing performance, seeking feedback from stakeholders, and staying informed about industry trends and best practices support a proactive approach to growth.

Leadership plays a pivotal role in guiding the business through the growth phase. Effective leaders provide a clear vision, set strategic priorities, and inspire and motivate the team. Strong leadership involves making informed decisions, managing resources effectively, and navigating challenges with confidence and resilience. Leaders must also communicate effectively, fostering a culture of transparency and collaboration. Supporting and developing leadership at all levels of the organization ensures that the business is well-equipped to manage growth and achieve its objectives.

In conclusion, scaling up a business sustainably involves a multifaceted approach that includes strategic planning, resource management, market analysis, and continuous improvement. Ensuring that the business infrastructure can support increased demand, securing necessary capital, and building a skilled and motivated workforce are critical components. Maintaining quality, leveraging technology, and adopting data-driven marketing and sales strategies enhance efficiency and reach. Innovation, strategic partnerships, and effective risk management drive growth and resilience. Sustainability, strong customer relationships, ethical practices, and flexible leadership underpin long-term success. By implementing these strategies, businesses can achieve sustainable growth and thrive in an increasingly competitive and dynamic market environment.

ppp

"Innovation and adaptation are key to staying ahead. Embrace change and continuously improve. Innovate to lead, adapt to survive."

EIGHTEEN

OVERCOMING CHALLENGES: NAVIGATING OBSTACLES WITH RESILIENCE

Navigating the obstacles that arise in business requires resilience, adaptability, and a strategic mindset. Every business, regardless of its size or industry, encounters challenges that can test its foundations and push its limits. These obstacles can range from financial difficulties, market fluctuations, and technological disruptions to internal conflicts, regulatory changes, and unforeseen crises. Overcoming these challenges necessitates a comprehensive approach that involves identifying problems, developing solutions, and fostering a resilient organizational culture.

The first step in overcoming challenges is recognizing and acknowledging them. It is crucial to maintain an open and transparent environment where issues can be identified and discussed without fear of blame or retribution. This involves fostering a culture where employees feel safe to speak up about problems and potential risks. Regularly assessing the business environment, both internal and external, helps identify emerging challenges early. This proactive approach allows for timely interventions and prevents minor issues from escalating into major crises.

Once challenges are identified, a thorough analysis is required to understand their root causes and potential impacts. This involves gathering and analyzing data, seeking input from relevant stakeholders, and considering different perspectives. Understanding the underlying factors contributing to a problem is essential for developing effective solutions. For example, financial difficulties might stem from declining sales, rising costs, or poor cash flow management. Identifying the specific causes allows for targeted strategies to address them.

Developing solutions requires creativity, strategic thinking, and a willingness to explore new approaches. It is important to consider multiple options and evaluate their feasibility, potential benefits, and risks. Involving a diverse group of employees in the problem-solving process can generate innovative ideas and foster a sense of ownership and commitment to the solutions. Scenario planning and contingency planning are valuable tools for preparing for different possible outcomes and ensuring that the business can respond effectively to various situations.

Resilience is a key attribute for navigating obstacles and overcoming challenges. Resilience involves the ability to adapt to changing circumstances, recover from setbacks, and continue moving forward. Building resilience within an organization involves fostering a positive and supportive culture, promoting mental and physical well-being, and providing opportunities for personal and professional development. Encouraging a growth mindset, where challenges are viewed as opportunities for learning and improvement, helps employees remain optimistic and motivated in the face of adversity.

Effective communication is critical for managing challenges and maintaining trust and morale within the organization. Clear and transparent communication ensures that employees are informed about the nature of the challenges, the strategies being implemented to address them, and their role in the process. Regular updates and open channels for feedback help keep everyone aligned and engaged. Communicating with external stakeholders, such as customers, suppliers, and investors, is also important for managing expectations and maintaining confidence in the business.

Financial challenges are among the most common obstacles businesses face. Managing financial difficulties requires a careful assessment of the company's financial health and the development of strategies to improve cash flow, reduce costs, and increase revenue. This may involve renegotiating payment terms with suppliers, securing additional funding, optimizing inventory management, and implementing cost-saving measures. It is also important to closely monitor financial performance and adjust strategies as needed to ensure long-term stability.

Market fluctuations and changes in consumer behavior can pose significant challenges for businesses. Staying attuned to market trends, customer preferences, and competitive dynamics is essential for anticipating and responding to these changes. Diversifying revenue streams, exploring new markets, and investing in market research can help mitigate the impact of market fluctuations. Flexibility and agility are crucial for adapting to changing market conditions and seizing new opportunities.

Technological disruptions can create both challenges and

opportunities for businesses. Keeping up with rapid technological advancements requires continuous learning and investment in new technologies. Embracing digital transformation can enhance efficiency, improve customer experiences, and create new business models. However, it also requires careful planning, resource allocation, and change management to ensure a smooth transition. Collaborating with technology partners, investing in employee training, and staying informed about industry developments can help businesses navigate technological disruptions effectively.

Internal conflicts and organizational issues can hinder performance and create obstacles to growth. Addressing these challenges involves promoting a positive and inclusive organizational culture, fostering open communication, and implementing effective conflict resolution mechanisms. Leadership plays a crucial role in setting the tone for the organization and modeling the behaviors and values that promote a harmonious and productive work environment. Providing opportunities for team-building, professional development, and employee engagement can strengthen relationships and enhance collaboration.

Regulatory changes and compliance requirements can present significant challenges, particularly in highly regulated industries. Staying informed about changes in laws and regulations, maintaining robust compliance programs, and seeking legal and regulatory advice are essential for navigating these challenges. Proactive engagement with regulators, industry associations, and other stakeholders can help businesses stay ahead of regulatory changes and advocate for favorable policies.

Unforeseen crises, such as natural disasters, pandemics, and geopolitical events, can have profound impacts on businesses. Crisis management involves developing and implementing plans to respond to emergencies, ensuring business continuity, and protecting employees, customers, and assets. A comprehensive crisis management plan includes risk assessment, contingency planning, communication strategies, and recovery procedures. Regularly reviewing and updating the plan, conducting drills and simulations, and learning from past crises can enhance preparedness and resilience.

Leadership is a critical factor in overcoming challenges and navigating obstacles. Effective leaders provide vision, direction, and inspiration, helping the organization stay focused and motivated during difficult times. They demonstrate empathy, resilience, and decisiveness, making tough decisions while considering the well-being of employees and other stakeholders. Strong leaders also foster a culture of accountability and empowerment, encouraging employees to take initiative and contribute to problem-solving efforts.

Continuous improvement and innovation are essential for staying competitive and overcoming challenges. Adopting a mindset of continuous improvement involves regularly evaluating processes, seeking feedback, and making incremental changes to enhance performance. Innovation requires creativity, experimentation, and a willingness to take risks. Encouraging a culture of innovation, providing resources for research and development, and recognizing and rewarding innovative ideas can drive continuous improvement and help businesses stay ahead of the curve.

Learning from failures and setbacks is a crucial aspect of resilience. Every challenge provides an opportunity to gain insights, develop new skills, and build stronger capabilities. Analyzing failures, understanding what went wrong, and applying those lessons to future efforts can lead to better decision-making and greater success. Celebrating small wins and milestones along the way helps maintain morale and momentum.

Building strong relationships with stakeholders, including

customers, employees, suppliers, and the community, enhances the ability to navigate challenges. Trust and collaboration are foundational to these relationships. Engaging with stakeholders, understanding their needs and concerns, and working together to find solutions create a supportive network that can provide valuable resources and assistance during challenging times.

Adopting a long-term perspective is important for sustainable success. While it is essential to address immediate challenges, businesses must also consider the long-term implications of their decisions and strategies. Balancing short-term pressures with long-term goals involves making strategic investments, planning for future growth, and building a resilient and adaptable organization. This long-term focus ensures that the business can weather challenges and continue to thrive in the future.

In conclusion, overcoming challenges and navigating obstacles with resilience requires a multifaceted approach that includes proactive identification and analysis of problems, creative problem-solving, effective communication, and strong leadership. Building a resilient organization involves fostering a positive culture, promoting continuous improvement, and leveraging innovation. Managing financial difficulties, adapting to market changes, embracing technological advancements, and addressing internal conflicts are all critical components. Staying informed about regulatory changes, preparing for unforeseen crises, and maintaining strong stakeholder relationships enhance the ability to navigate challenges. By adopting these strategies and maintaining a long-term perspective, businesses can overcome obstacles, build resilience, and achieve sustainable success.

ϷϷϷ

"Celebrate milestones to acknowledge hard work and dedication. Reflect on achievements and plan for the future. Success is a journey, not a destination."

NINETEEN

INNOVATION AND ADAPTATION: STAYING AHEAD IN THE MARKET

In the dynamic and competitive landscape of modern business, innovation and adaptation are crucial for staying ahead in the market. Companies that prioritize these elements are better equipped to navigate challenges, seize opportunities, and drive long-term success. Innovation involves creating and implementing new ideas, processes, products, or services that add value. Adaptation, on the other hand, refers to the ability to adjust to changes in the market environment, consumer behavior, and technological advancements. Both are interdependent and essential for maintaining a competitive edge.

The starting point for fostering innovation is cultivating a culture that encourages creativity and risk-taking. A supportive environment where employees feel empowered to experiment and explore new ideas is vital. This involves providing the necessary resources, such as time, funding, and tools, and creating a safe space for trial and error. Recognizing and rewarding innovative efforts, even if they fail, reinforces the importance of innovation and encourages continuous efforts. Leadership plays a critical role in setting the tone for this culture, demonstrating a commitment to innovation, and leading by example.

Collaboration is a key driver of innovation. Bringing together diverse teams with varied skills, experiences, and perspectives can lead to more creative and effective solutions. Cross-functional collaboration, where employees from different departments work together on projects, fosters a holistic approach to problem-solving and innovation. Open communication and the sharing of ideas are essential for this collaboration to thrive. Regular brainstorming sessions, innovation workshops, and hackathons can provide structured opportunities for teams to collaborate and generate new ideas.

Customer-centricity is another important aspect of innovation. Understanding customer needs, preferences, and pain points provides valuable insights that can drive the development of new products and services. Engaging with customers through surveys, focus groups, and social media can help identify unmet needs and opportunities for improvement. Co-creation, where customers are involved in the development process, ensures that the final product or service is closely aligned with their expectations. This approach not only leads to more relevant innovations but also fosters stronger customer relationships and loyalty.

Leveraging technology is crucial for driving innovation and adaptation. Rapid advancements in technology present both opportunities and challenges for businesses. Staying ahead requires a proactive approach to adopting new technologies and integrating them into business processes. This includes investing in research and development, exploring emerging technologies such as artificial intelligence, machine learning, blockchain, and the

Internet of Things, and continuously upgrading existing systems and infrastructure. Technology can enhance efficiency, improve customer experiences, and open up new business models and revenue streams.

Data analytics is a powerful tool for innovation and adaptation. Analyzing data from various sources, such as customer interactions, market trends, and operational performance, provides actionable insights that can inform decision-making and strategy. Predictive analytics can help forecast future trends and identify potential opportunities and risks. By leveraging data, businesses can make more informed and agile decisions, optimize processes, and personalize customer experiences. Ensuring data quality and security is essential for maximizing the value of data analytics.

Agility is a critical attribute for adaptation. Businesses need to be able to respond quickly and effectively to changes in the market environment. This requires a flexible organizational structure, streamlined decision-making processes, and the ability to pivot and adjust strategies as needed. Agile methodologies, such as Scrum and Kanban, provide frameworks for managing projects and processes in a way that enhances flexibility and responsiveness. These methodologies emphasize iterative development, continuous feedback, and collaboration, enabling teams to adapt to changing requirements and deliver value more quickly.

Continuous learning and development are essential for maintaining a competitive edge. The rapid pace of change in the market and technology means that skills and knowledge can quickly become outdated. Encouraging and supporting ongoing education, training, and professional development ensures that employees remain competent and capable of driving innovation and adaptation. This can include formal training programs, workshops, online courses, and attending industry conferences. Fostering a learning culture where employees are encouraged to seek out new knowledge and share their learnings with others enhances the overall capability of the organization.

Strategic partnerships and alliances can also drive innovation and adaptation. Collaborating with other businesses, startups, research institutions, and industry organizations can provide access to new ideas, technologies, and markets. Partnerships can take various forms, such as joint ventures, strategic alliances, and research collaborations. By leveraging the strengths and expertise of partners, businesses can accelerate innovation, reduce costs, and enhance their competitive position. It is important to carefully select partners whose values, goals, and capabilities align with those of the business.

Adapting to changes in consumer behavior is crucial for staying ahead in the market. Shifts in consumer preferences, values, and purchasing habits can significantly impact demand for products and services. Keeping a pulse on these changes through market research, customer feedback, and social media monitoring helps businesses anticipate and respond to evolving needs. Personalization and customization of products and services to meet individual preferences can enhance customer satisfaction and loyalty. Flexibility in pricing, distribution, and marketing strategies allows businesses to adapt to changing consumer behavior effectively.

Regulatory changes and compliance requirements can pose challenges for businesses, but they also present opportunities for innovation. Staying informed about changes in laws and regulations, engaging with regulatory bodies, and proactively addressing compliance issues can enhance the business's reputation and reduce risks. Innovations in compliance processes, such as using technology for automated monitoring and reporting, can improve efficiency and accuracy. Businesses that navigate regulatory changes effectively can also differentiate themselves by demonstrating a commitment to ethical and responsible practices.

Sustainability and corporate social responsibility (CSR) are increasingly important factors for innovation and adaptation. Consumers, investors, and other stakeholders are placing greater emphasis on environmental and social impacts. Integrating sustainability into business strategy involves adopting practices that minimize negative impacts and contribute positively to society and the environment. This can include reducing waste and emissions, sourcing materials responsibly, and supporting community initiatives. Innovations in sustainable products, processes, and business models can drive competitive advantage and align the business with the values of its stakeholders.

Monitoring and evaluating the impact of innovation and adaptation efforts are essential for continuous improvement. Setting clear goals and metrics for innovation initiatives, regularly reviewing progress, and assessing outcomes provide valuable insights into what is working and what needs adjustment. Feedback loops, where learnings from one project inform future efforts, enhance the effectiveness of innovation processes. Celebrating successes and recognizing contributions to innovation reinforce the importance of these efforts and motivate continued engagement.

Leadership is a critical factor in driving innovation and adaptation. Leaders set the vision, create the conditions for innovation, and inspire and motivate the team. Effective leaders demonstrate a commitment to innovation, embrace change, and encourage experimentation. They provide strategic direction while empowering employees to take initiative and make decisions. Leading by example, being open to new ideas, and fostering a culture of trust and collaboration are key leadership attributes for fostering innovation and adaptation.

In conclusion, staying ahead in the market requires a dual focus on innovation and adaptation. Cultivating a culture that encourages creativity, collaboration, and risk-taking is essential for driving innovation. Leveraging technology, data analytics, and continuous learning enhances the ability to innovate and adapt. Flexibility, agility, and strategic partnerships enable businesses to respond effectively to market changes. Adapting to evolving consumer behavior, regulatory changes, and sustainability trends ensures long-term relevance and success. Effective leadership and continuous monitoring and evaluation support sustained innovation and adaptation. By prioritizing these elements, businesses can navigate challenges, seize opportunities, and maintain a competitive edge in the dynamic market landscape.

ppp

"Effective leadership guides the organization through change. Inspire and motivate your team. Lead with vision, integrity, and resilience."

TWENTY

REFLECTING ON SUCCESS: CELEBRATING MILESTONES AND PLANNING AHEAD

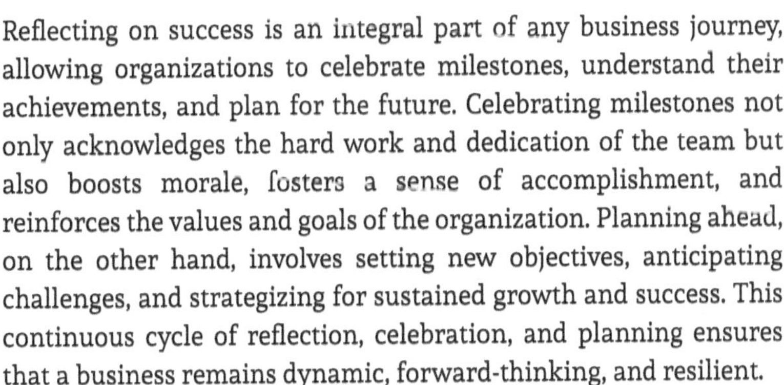

Reflecting on success is an integral part of any business journey, allowing organizations to celebrate milestones, understand their achievements, and plan for the future. Celebrating milestones not only acknowledges the hard work and dedication of the team but also boosts morale, fosters a sense of accomplishment, and reinforces the values and goals of the organization. Planning ahead, on the other hand, involves setting new objectives, anticipating challenges, and strategizing for sustained growth and success. This continuous cycle of reflection, celebration, and planning ensures that a business remains dynamic, forward-thinking, and resilient.

Success in business is often measured by key milestones, which can include reaching financial targets, launching new products, expanding into new markets, achieving customer satisfaction goals, or hitting significant anniversaries. Recognizing these milestones provides an opportunity to pause and reflect on what has been accomplished. It is important to consider not only the end results but also the processes, strategies, and collaborative efforts that contributed to these achievements. This holistic reflection allows for a deeper understanding of what works well and what could be improved, providing valuable insights for future endeavors.

Celebrating milestones is an important way to acknowledge and reward the contributions of employees, who are the backbone of any successful organization. Celebrations can take various forms, from formal events such as award ceremonies and gala dinners to informal gatherings like team lunches and office parties. These occasions provide a platform to publicly recognize individual and team achievements, fostering a culture of appreciation and motivation. Public recognition, such as employee of the month awards, can boost morale and encourage a sense of pride and ownership in one's work. Additionally, celebrating milestones can strengthen team cohesion, as employees share in the collective success and feel more connected to the organization's goals and values.

Beyond internal celebrations, sharing success stories with external stakeholders such as customers, partners, and investors can enhance the organization's reputation and build stronger relationships. Press releases, social media announcements, and newsletters can be used to communicate achievements and milestones, showcasing the organization's progress and reinforcing its credibility and reliability. Transparency in sharing both successes and the journey to achieve them can build trust and loyalty among stakeholders, who appreciate the organization's commitment to excellence and continuous improvement.

While celebrating success is important, it is equally crucial to use these moments as an opportunity for reflection and learning. Analyzing the factors that contributed to success can help identify best practices, effective strategies, and key strengths that can be leveraged in future projects. This involves gathering feedback from employees, customers, and other stakeholders to gain different perspectives on what worked well and why. Understanding the enablers of success allows the organization to replicate and scale these practices, driving further achievements.

At the same time, reflection should also include an honest assessment of any challenges or setbacks encountered along the way. Identifying areas for improvement and learning from mistakes is essential for growth and resilience. This process of continuous learning and adaptation ensures that the organization remains agile and better prepared to navigate future challenges. Encouraging a culture where employees feel safe to discuss failures and lessons learned fosters innovation and risk-taking, which are critical for long-term success.

Planning ahead is the next logical step after reflecting on success. Setting new goals and objectives based on the insights gained from past achievements and lessons learned helps maintain momentum and drives the organization forward. Strategic planning involves analyzing current market trends, competitive dynamics, and internal capabilities to identify opportunities for growth and areas for improvement. This forward-looking approach ensures that the organization remains proactive and aligned with its long-term vision and mission.

Goal setting should be a collaborative process that involves input from various stakeholders, including employees, management, and external partners. This inclusive approach ensures that the goals are realistic, achievable, and aligned with the needs and aspirations of the organization and its stakeholders. Setting SMART goals (Specific, Measurable, Achievable, Relevant, Time-bound) provides a clear framework for planning and tracking progress. These goals should be broken down into actionable steps, with assigned responsibilities and timelines to ensure accountability and execution.

Anticipating challenges and potential obstacles is a critical aspect of planning ahead. This involves conducting a thorough risk assessment to identify and mitigate potential risks that could impact the organization's objectives. Developing contingency plans and building flexibility into the strategic plan allows the organization to respond effectively to unforeseen circumstances. Regularly reviewing and updating the risk management plan ensures that it remains relevant and robust in the face of changing conditions.

Innovation and continuous improvement should be integral components of the strategic plan. Staying ahead in a competitive market requires a commitment to innovation, whether through developing new products and services, enhancing existing offerings, or improving operational efficiencies. Encouraging a culture of continuous improvement involves regularly reviewing processes, seeking feedback, and making incremental changes to enhance performance. Investing in research and development, embracing new technologies, and fostering a mindset of experimentation and learning are essential for driving innovation and sustaining growth.

Effective communication is crucial for aligning the organization around the strategic plan and ensuring that everyone is working towards the same goals. Clear and transparent communication helps build understanding, commitment, and motivation among employees. Regular updates on progress, achievements, and any changes to the plan keep everyone informed and engaged. Providing opportunities for employees to share their ideas, feedback, and concerns ensures that the plan remains dynamic and responsive to the needs of the organization.

Leadership plays a pivotal role in driving the strategic plan and ensuring its successful execution. Effective leaders provide vision, direction, and inspiration, helping the organization navigate challenges and seize opportunities. They demonstrate resilience, adaptability, and a commitment to continuous learning and improvement. By fostering a positive and inclusive organizational culture, leaders can create an environment where employees feel valued, supported, and empowered to contribute to the organization's success.

Monitoring and evaluating progress towards the strategic goals is essential for staying on track and making necessary adjustments. This involves regularly reviewing key performance indicators (KPIs) and other metrics to assess performance and identify any deviations from the plan. Using data and analytics to inform decision-making provides a more objective and accurate picture of progress. Regular progress reviews and performance assessments allow for timely interventions and course corrections, ensuring that the organization remains aligned with its goals.

Celebrating milestones along the way is important for maintaining motivation and momentum. Recognizing and rewarding achievements, both big and small, reinforces the organization's commitment to excellence and continuous improvement. These celebrations provide an opportunity to reflect on progress, acknowledge contributions, and renew focus and energy for the next phase of the journey.

In conclusion, reflecting on success, celebrating milestones, and planning ahead are essential components of a dynamic and forward-thinking business strategy. Celebrating milestones acknowledges the hard work and dedication of the team, boosts morale, and strengthens the organizational culture. Reflection provides valuable insights into what works well and what can be improved, driving continuous learning and adaptation. Planning ahead ensures that the organization remains proactive, aligned with its long-term vision, and prepared for future challenges and opportunities. By integrating these elements into their strategic approach, businesses can achieve sustained growth, resilience, and success in an ever-changing market landscape.

ᐯᐯᐯ

"Reflecting on success provides insights for future growth. Celebrate, learn, and plan ahead. A successful business is always evolving."

TWENTY-ONE
SUMMARY

Reflecting on the journey of building and growing a successful business involves understanding various key elements that contribute to sustainability, growth, and long-term success. This summary chapter brings together insights from previous discussions on entrepreneurship, vision crafting, market research, business planning, legal foundations, funding, brand identity, digital presence, product development, pricing strategies, marketing tactics, sales techniques, customer service, operational efficiency, team building, financial management, scaling up, overcoming challenges, and innovation and adaptation. Each of these elements plays a crucial role in the business lifecycle, guiding entrepreneurs through the complexities of establishing and nurturing their ventures.

Entrepreneurship begins with a vision, an idea that sparks the journey towards building a business. Crafting a clear and compelling vision is essential as it defines the direction and purpose of the business. This vision must be backed by thorough market research to understand the target audience, competitors, and industry trends. Market research provides the insights needed to refine the business idea, ensuring it meets the needs of the market and stands out from the competition.

A well-structured business plan is the blueprint for success, outlining the strategy for achieving business goals. It covers various aspects including the business model, marketing strategy, financial projections, and operational plans. A robust business plan not only helps in securing funding but also serves as a roadmap for the business's growth and development. Legal foundations, such as business registration, intellectual property protection, and compliance with regulations, are critical to establishing a secure and credible business structure.

Funding is often one of the biggest challenges for new ventures. Exploring various financing options, from personal savings and angel investors to venture capital and crowdfunding, is essential for securing the necessary capital. Each funding source has its own set of advantages and considerations, and entrepreneurs must carefully evaluate them to choose the best fit for their business needs. Effective financial management ensures that the business remains profitable and sustainable, with careful budgeting, forecasting, and cash flow management.

Creating a memorable brand identity helps in differentiating the business and building a loyal customer base. This involves developing a cohesive visual identity, crafting a compelling brand message, and consistently communicating the brand across all touchpoints. A strong digital presence is crucial in today's market, leveraging websites, social media, SEO, and digital marketing to reach and engage with the target audience.

Product development is the process of bringing the business idea to life. This involves ideation, design, prototyping, testing, and refining the product to meet customer needs and market demands. Effective pricing strategies ensure that the product is competitively positioned while maintaining profitability. Pricing decisions should consider factors such as cost, value to the customer, competition, and market conditions.

Marketing tactics are essential for reaching and engaging the target market. This involves a mix of digital and traditional marketing channels, content marketing, social media engagement, email marketing, and paid advertising. Sales techniques focus on converting leads into customers through effective communication, relationship building, and closing strategies. Providing excellent customer service builds loyalty and retention, creating a positive customer experience and fostering long-term relationships.

Operational efficiency involves streamlining processes to reduce waste, improve productivity, and enhance overall performance. This requires continuous assessment and optimization of workflows, technology integration, and employee engagement. Building a strong team is crucial for achieving business goals, involving effective hiring, training, and management practices. A positive organizational culture, clear communication, and recognition of achievements contribute to a motivated and high-performing team.

Financial management is a cornerstone of business sustainability, involving careful planning, budgeting, forecasting, and monitoring of financial performance. Effective cash flow management, investment decisions, cost control, and risk management are essential for maintaining profitability and growth. Scaling up the business involves expanding operations, increasing revenue, and entering new markets. This requires strategic planning, resource management, and maintaining the quality and core values of the business.

Overcoming challenges and navigating obstacles with resilience is part of the business journey. This involves identifying problems, developing solutions, and fostering a resilient organizational culture. Effective communication, financial management, adaptability, and continuous improvement are key to overcoming challenges. Innovation and adaptation are crucial for staying ahead in the market, involving a culture of creativity, customer-centricity, technology integration, and continuous learning.

Reflecting on success involves celebrating milestones, recognizing achievements, and planning ahead. Celebrating milestones boosts morale and strengthens the organizational culture, while reflection provides insights for continuous improvement. Planning ahead involves setting new goals, anticipating challenges, and strategizing for sustained growth. Leadership plays a critical role in guiding the organization through these processes, providing vision, direction, and inspiration.

In conclusion, the journey of building and growing a successful business is multifaceted, involving a combination of strategic planning, effective management, innovation, and adaptability. Each element, from entrepreneurship and vision crafting to financial management and scaling up, plays a crucial role in ensuring the sustainability and growth of the business. By integrating these elements into their strategic approach, businesses can navigate challenges, seize opportunities, and achieve long-term success in an ever-changing market landscape. Reflecting on success, celebrating milestones, and planning ahead are essential components of this journey, ensuring that businesses remain dynamic, forward-thinking, and resilient.

ᗧᗧᗧ

Citation And References

This book represents the culmination of extensive research and meticulous analysis, incorporating a diverse range of sources, including numerous books, scholarly studies, and personal experiences. Additionally, I have scoured various websites to gather relevant information and data essential for the compilation of this work. I have taken every precaution to ensure the accuracy of the information presented and have diligently cited all sources to acknowledge their contributions.

Despite these efforts, the possibility of inadvertent errors remains. I deeply value the insights of my readers and appreciate any feedback that can help identify and rectify such inaccuracies. I encourage you to bring any discrepancies to my attention.

Your feedback is not only welcome but crucial, as it will aid in correcting current editions and enhancing the content of future ones. I am committed to maintaining the highest standards of accuracy and reliability in my work and thank you for your support and understanding.

Additionally, I firmly uphold the principle of freedom of speech and expression as guaranteed under Article 19(1)(a) of the Constitution of India, and I respect the diverse viewpoints and expressions of all readers.

ϷϷϷ

Other Books Of The Author

1. Empowering Minds: A Journey into Women's Self-Discovery and Power
2. The Dynamics of Motivation: Catalyzing Thought into Action
3. Meditation and Mental Well Being: The Path to Inner Peace and Clarity
4. The Psychology of Child Education: Nurturing Future Generations
5. Ethical Enlightenment: A Modern Guide to Living with Integrity
6. Voices of Empowerment: Stories of Women Rising Against Odds
7. Social Psychology in Everyday Life: Understanding Human Connections
8. The Essence of Motivational Speaking: Inspiring Change in Others
9. Balancing Acts: Women, Work, and the Will to Lead
10. Guiding with Grace: Raising Children with Compassion and Awareness
11. The Power of Positive Aging: Embracing Life After Fifty
12. Building Resilient Communities: Social Work in Action
13. The Ethical Educator: Principles for Teaching and Learning
14. From Insight to Impact: Social Psychology for a Better World
15. The Ethics of Empathy: A Guide to Ethical Living
16. The Science of Empowering the Self: Navigating Life's Challenges with Psychological Wisdom
17. The Mindful Conscious Leader: Meditation Techniques for Modern Management
18. Pioneering Spirit: Women's Pathways to Leadership and Empowerment
19. Feeling to Healing: The Role of Emotional Intelligence in Child Development
20. Transformative Talks and Words of Inspiration: Insights into Motivational Oratory

21. Green Ethics: A Path to Sustainable Living
22. Spiritual Integrity: Navigating Life with Moral Compassion
23. Clean Living, Clean Society: The Ethics of Cleanliness
24. Patriotic Spirits: Building a Nation on Positive Attitudes
25. Innovative Integrity & Vibrant Visions: The Ethical and Entrepreneurial Spirit of Gujarat
26. Youthful Visions, Endless Possibilities: Inspiring Ethics and Motivation in Children
27. Living Your Legacy: How to Motivate Others by Living Your Values
28. Secret of Healing Conversations: Ethical Practices in Counselling and Therapy
29. Creative Kindness: Crafting a Life of Compassion and Creativity
30. The Power of Appreciation: How Gratitude Can Transform Your Relationships
31. Bhagavad-Gita: Messages
32. Science of Art: The New Frontier of Fashion Modernism
33. Vivekananda's Virtues: A Blueprint for Modern Living
34. Empower Her: Navigating the Path to Women's Entrepreneurship
35. The Boundless Classroom: Innovations in Global Education
36. The Language of Leadership: Communicating with Authenticity and Impact
37. The Warrior's Mantra: Deciphering the Hanuman Chalisa
38. Echoes of Empathy: Transformative Stories of Social Service
39. Artful Living: Cultivating Creativity in Your Daily Routine
40. Finding Your Why: Discovering Your Passions and Charting Your Course
41. The Role of Social Media in Shaping Self-Esteem and Interpersonal Relationships among Adolescents
42. Karma's Tapestry: Weaving a Life of Selfless Service
43. Altruistic Alchemy: Transforming Lives Through Giving
44. The Blueprint of Pro-Activeness and Productivity: Crafting Habits for Success
45. The Simplicity with Grounded Wisdom: Embracing Authenticity

in a Complex World

46. Secret of Solopreneur's Odyssey: Navigating the Path to Self-Employment
47. Exploring Tapestry of Peace: Global Perspectives on Harmony
48. The Art and Actions of Connection: Mastering Communication for Impact
49. She Governs and at the Helm: Strategies for Political Empowerment
50. Rising Above and Rising with Grace: A Woman's Roadmap to Career Mastery
51. The Effect of Networking & Connectedness: Building Strategic Alliances for Women
52. Beyond his Barriers: Women Thriving in Male-Dominated Fields
53. Secret of Inner Compass: Navigating Life with Intuition
54. Creative & Pro-Active Muses: A Celebration of Women in the Arts
55. Unburdened: The Art of Releasing the Past
56. Amplified Voices: Speeches of Women that Astonished the World
57. Secret of Manifesting Dreams: A Woman's Guide to Intentional Living
58. Ethics and Value Based Education: Reimagining Japan's School System
59. The Moral Compass Curriculum: A Holistic Approach
60. Tech with Heart: Integrating Ethics into Digital Learning
61. Honoring Virtue: Recognizing Ethical Excellence in Education
62. Raising Good Humans: A Guide to Character Development
63. The Spark Within: Nurturing Creativity in Children
64. The Teenager Whisperer: Navigating Adolescence with Grace
65. Igniting a Passion for Learning: Inspiring Lifelong Curiosity
66. The Habit Lab: Cultivating Positive Behaviors in Children
67. Seeds of Empathy: Fostering Compassion in Young Hearts
68. The Reading Revolution: Inspiring a Love of Books in Children
69. The Learning Brain: Unlocking the Secrets of Student Success
70. Teaching for All: Differentiated Instruction Strategies
71. The Time Alchemist: Mastering Time Management for Peak Performance

Bhajan

101. Pilgrimage of the Soul: Spiritual Journeys in India

༺༺༺

Contact

Dr. Minakshi Bansal
Social Activist
Ahmedabad, Gujarat, Bharat
minakshiindiag20@yahoo.com

❧❧❧

|| LOKAHA SAMASTHAHA SUKHINO BHAVANTU ||